2

LEGAL DEVELOPMENT IN COLONIAL MASSACHUSETTS

STUDIES IN HISTORY, ECONOMICS AND PUBLIC LAW

EDITED BY THE FACULTY OF POLITICAL SCIENCE OF
COLUMBIA UNIVERSITY

Volume XXXVII] [Number 2

Whole Number 98

LEGAL DEVELOPMENT

IN

COLONIAL MASSACHUSETTS

1630-1686

BY

CHARLES J. HILKEY

AMS Press, Inc.
New York
1967

AMS Press, Inc.
New York, N.Y. 10003
1967

Manufactured in the United States of America

PREFACE

According to the accepted legal theory, the American colonists claimed the English common law as their birthright, brought with them its general principles and adopted so much of it as was applicable to their condition. Although this theory is universally adopted by the courts, a close study of the subject reveals among the early colonists a far different attitude toward the common law from that which is usually attributed to them. In none of the colonies, perhaps, was this more marked than in early Massachusetts. Here the binding force of English law was denied, and a legal system largely different came into use. It is the purpose of this work to trace the development of that system during the period of the first charter. In a few instances the material is of such a nature that it was found advisable to invert the logical order of presentation, but it is believed that the reasons for this will be clear to the reader.

The writer wishes to express his appreciation for assistance in his earlier investigations rendered by Professors J. W. Burgess and H. L. Osgood, of Columbia, and by Professor W. C. Abbott, of Yale. Special thanks are due to Professor Munroe Smith, of Columbia, for valuable aid and suggestions in the preparation and arrangement of the material.

It is the writer's hope to enlarge upon the present work at some future time and to carry it down to the American Revolution.

CONTENTS

CHAPTER I

The Law-making Factors

CHAPTER I

The Law-Making Factors

THE LEGISLATIVE DEPARTMENT

The history of the law-making factors of Massachusetts begins properly with the charter granted March 4, 1628.[1] This royal charter both confirmed the grant obtained from the Council for New England, March 19, 1627, and added to it certain governmental powers.[2] A corporation was created by the name of the "Governor and Company of the Massachusetts Bay in New England."[3] There were to be a governor, a deputy-governor, and eighteen assistants, chosen from the members of the corporation. The governor, or, in his absence, the deputy-governor, had authority to give order for assembling the company. Once every month, or oftener at their pleasure, the governor, deputy-governor, and assistants were to hold a court, and seven assistants with the governor, or deputy, were to constitute a quorum. This body was empowered to transact such business as should come up concerning the company or plantation. Aside from this, the governor or deputy-governor, and

[1] Dates old style.

[2] Macdonald, *Select Charters and Other Documents* (New York, 1904), p. 37.

[3] Text of charter in Poore, *The Federal and State Constitutions, Colonial Charters and other Organic Laws* (Washington, 1878), pt. i, pp. 932-42.

seven or more of the assistants were to hold upon the last "Wednesday in Hillary, Easter, Trinity and Michas Terms," a general assembly. These were styled "the Four Great and General Courts of the Company." The governor, or deputy, seven assistants, and as many freemen as should be present constituted a quorum. Thus assembled, the greater number of those present, which majority was always to include the governor, or deputy, and at least six assistants, had power to admit freemen, elect officers, and make laws and ordinances, not repugnant to those of England. The governor, deputy-governor, assistants, and all other officers of the company were to be elected every year at the General Court held the last Wednesday in Easter term.[1]

Besides the provision that the laws passed by the General Court were not to be repugnant to those of England, there was another restriction. All British subjects were to have the same liberties and immunities as if in England.[2]

Such was the governmental power granted to the company. It is very likely that the crown intended to constitute, by the charter, a corporation in England, similar to the East India and other great companies, with power to settle plantations within the limits of its territory, under such forms of government and magistracy as should be necessary.[3] But this point was not settled by charter,[4] and it seems that some of the members of the company had another view in mind, or at least soon

[1] Poore, pt. i, p. 937.

[2] *Ibid.*, pt. i, p. 940.

[3] Hutchinson, *The History of the Colony of Massachusetts Bay* (London, 1765), vol. i, p. 13.

[4] Osgood, *The American Colonies in the Seventeenth Century* (New York, 1904-7), vol. i, p. 143.

conceived that another plan would be possible.[1] The first indication of this in the records is found in the proceedings of the General Court held in England, July 28, 1629. Here Cradock, the governor,

read certain propositions conceived by himself, viz.: that for the advancement of the plantation, the inducing and encouraging persons of worth and quality to transplant themselves and families thither, and for other weighty reasons therein contained, [it is expedient] to transfer the government of the plantation to those that shall inhabit there, and not to continue the same in subordination to the company here, as now it is.

The question was debated at some length, but was not decided at that Court. Those present, however, were to consider the matter thoroughly and to set down in writing arguments both pro and con and to produce them at the next General Court, when the company was to make a final decision upon the matter. The whole affair, till the next meeting, was to be carried on in secret.[2] But two days before the next session twelve gentlemen, among whom were Thomas Dudley, Isaac Johnson and John Winthrop, met at Cambridge and entered into a written agreement that they would remove with their families to America, provided an arrangement should be made by which the government and patent would be transferred thither.[3] At the next meeting, August 28,

[1] Palfrey, *History of New England* (Boston, 1858–90), vol. i, pp. 306–7; Hubbard, *A General History of New England* (Mass. Hist. Colls., 2nd Ser., vols. v, vi), p. 108; Johnson, *Wonder-Working Providence*, Mass. Hist. Colls., 2nd Ser., vol. ii, p. 53.

[2] *Massachusetts Colonial Records* (ed. by Shurtleff, Boston, 1850–54), vol. i, p. 49; Palfrey, vol. i, pp. 301–2.

[3] Young, *Chronicles* (Boston, 1846), pp. 281–2; Palfrey, vol. i, p. 302.

1629, the deputy-governor informed the court that the special cause for the session was to give answer to divers gentlemen, intending to go to New England, whether or not the chief government of the plantation, together with the patent, would be settled there. It was decided that two committees should be appointed, one to consider arguments in favor of, and the other arguments against the transfer. The two committees were to meet at seven the next morning, and were to confer and report at nine to the whole company, who should then settle the question.[1] The result was that the court met next morning and voted to transfer both the government and patent to New England.[2]

This decision made necessary a new choice of officers, which took place at the General Court, October 20, 1629. John Winthrop was chosen governor and John Humphry deputy-governor; assistants were also elected.[3] Various other arrangements were made for the transfer,[4] and the company's government on the other side of the water soon drew to a close. The last meeting of the General Court was held February 10, 1629,[5] and the last meeting of the court of assistants took place aboard the Arbella the 23d of the following month.[6] The latter part of March, Winthrop and a large company with him left England for America.[7]

[1] *Mass. Col. Rec.*, vol. i, p. 48.

[2] *Ibid.*, vol. i, p. 51; Palfrey, vol. i, p. 302; Hutchinson, vol. i, pp. 12-13; Hubbard, pp. 123-4.

[3] *Mass. Col. Rec.*, vol. i, p. 59; Palfrey, vol. i, pp. 302-3.

[4] *Mass. Col. Rec.*, vol. i, pp. 51-70.

[5] *Ibid.*, vol. i, p. 67.

[6] *Ibid.*, vol. i, p. 70.

[7] Letter to his wife, Winthrop (ed. by Savage, Boston, 1853), vol. i, pp. 441-2.

Prior to this time a local government had been established at Salem under John Endicott, styled "London's Plantation in Massachusetts Bay in New England."[1] But of course this government was superseded by that of the company as soon as the transfer was actually accomplished.

The first court of assistants in America was held August 23, 1630,[2] at "Charlton," and the General Court convened for the first time at Boston the 19th day of the following October.[3] From the beginning the court of assistants exercised a sort of general legislative and judicial power. At its second meeting, held September 7, it was agreed that a court should be held every third Tuesday at the governor's house.[4] At the same time it was ordered that Thomas Morton should be presently set in the "bilbowes" and, after being sent prisoner to England, all his goods were to be seized to defray his transportation, pay his debts, and give satisfaction to the Indians for a canoe he had taken from them; also his house was to be burned down in sight of the Indians to their satisfaction for the many wrongs he had from time to time done them. Besides this, a number of other orders were passed. A judgment was rendered in favor of a plaintiff, an appropriation was made, and some of the towns were named. The next court, held September 28, issued similar orders.[5]

Such was the authority assumed by the assistants when the General Court assembled. The purpose of this meeting, as stated by the Court itself, was to establish the government. The power already exercised by the

[1] Macdonald, *Charters*, p. 37; *Mass. Col. Rec.*, vol. i, p. 361.
[2] *Ibid.*, vol. i, p. 73.
[3] *Ibid.*, vol. i, p. 79.
[4] *Ibid.*, vol. i, p. 75.
[5] *Ibid.*, vol. i, pp. 76-7.

court of assistants was virtually confirmed. It was agreed that the freemen should choose assistants, and that the assistants should choose from among their own number the governor and the deputy-governor. So constituted, that body was to make laws and appoint officers to execute them.[1] Thus at their first meeting did the freemen surrender a large part of the power granted them by the charter. The assistants, on the other hand, did not hesitate in assuming the responsibility. They even went so far, in their meeting held March 8, 1630, as to declare, contrary to the charter, that, whenever the number of assistants within the colony should be fewer than nine, the major part of them could hold a valid court. The reason assigned for this order was that the number was few and some were going back to England.[2] But the absolute necessity of such an arrangement is not clear, since the court of elections was little more than two months off. But it is very probable that the assistants neither looked with favor upon the elections, nor even saw the need of them.

The first opposition to the growing power of the assistants appeared in the General Court held May 18, 1631. Here the governor and deputy-governor were elected in the usual way, in complete disregard of the order of the previous year delegating that power to the assistants. The records of this election indicate that the charter had been consulted, since it is stated that John Winthrop was elected governor for the next year by the general consent of the Court, according to the meaning of the patent. The Court went still further and declared that there should be at least one General Court held

[1] *Mass. Col. Rec.*, vol, i, p. 79.

[2] *Ibid.*, vol. i, p. 84.

each year for the freemen to elect and remove assistants.[1] From this time on there was a marked struggle between the aristocratic tendencies on the part of the assistants and the democratic demands made by the people. The General Court was the common body in which these two elements met and strove for supremacy.

Among the various powers claimed by the assistants was that of taxation. This right was questioned by some of the freemen of Watertown. A tax had been levied, February 3, 1631, for the purpose of fortifying Newtown, and Watertown's part of that levy was eight pounds. But the pastor and elder assembled the people and told them that they did not think it safe to pay money in that way, for fear they might bring themselves and posterity into bondage. The ground of their protest was that they looked upon the magistrates as similar to a mayor and aldermen, who had no power to make laws or raise taxes without the people. February 17th, a number of the Watertown freemen were called before the governor and magistrates and informed that the court of assistants was more in the nature of a parliament, and that no assistant could be chosen except by the freemen, who also had power to remove them and put in others, and that at every General Court they were at liberty to declare their grievances. This explanation seemed to satisfy the protesting party, and their submission was accepted by the court and their offense pardoned.[2]

At a meeting held March 6, 1631, the court of assistants changed the time of its sessions to the first Tuesday in every month. It also ordered that no planter, re-

[1] *Mass. Col. Rec.*, vol. i, p. 87.

[2] Winthrop (Savage), vol. i. p. 84.

turning to England, should carry with him either money or beaver, without leave from the governor, under pain of their forfeiture.[1] At the next meeting, held May 1, 1632, the assistants received information of some measures which were to be demanded by the freemen. This seems to have been a private session, since no report of it is given in the records. After dinner the governor told them he had heard that the people were going to request, at the next General Court, that the assistants might be chosen anew every year and that the governor might be chosen by the whole Court in place of the assistants only. Upon this communication, Mr. Ludlow fell in a passion and said that they would then have no government, but that there would be an interim when every man might do as he pleased. This was cleared in the minds of the other assistants, but Ludlow still held to his opinion and declared that he would return to England if the people carried out their purpose.[2]

The General Court met May 9 and ordered that the governor, deputy-governor, and assistants should be chosen by the whole Court, which was to include the above-named officers and the freemen. But the governor was always to be chosen from the assistants. Then, in regard to taxation, it was provided that there should be two of each plantation appointed to confer with the governor and assistants concerning methods of raising public stock.[3]

This last arrangement seems to have been the beginning of the representative system in the colony. Be this as it may, that system was soon to make its appearance.

[1] *Mass. Col. Rec.*, vol. i, p. 93.

[2] Winthrop (Savage), vol. i, p. 88.

[3] *Mass. Col. Rec.*, vol. i, p. 95; Winthrop (Savage), vol. i, pp. 90–1.

Notice was sent out for a General Court to be held in May, 1634. The freemen of each town deputed two of their number to meet and consider the things upon which they were to take action. These delegates assembled and, after looking over the patent, discovered that all the laws should be made at the General Court. They went to confer with the governor about this point and about the abrogation of certain orders concerning swine, which had been made by the court of assistants.[1] Here they were reminded of the large number of freemen, the scattered settlements, and the impracticability of assembling to make laws under the existing conditions of the colony. The governor, however, suggested that for the present they might make an order at the General Court that once in the year a certain number should be chosen, upon summons from the governor, to revise all laws and reform what they found amiss therein. He intimated, moreover, that these delegates should be limited a great deal in power.[2] How well the last suggestion was followed is shown by what took place during the next few weeks.

The towns were not slow in putting the governor's plan of representation into practice. The first General Court of which the deputies composed a part met May 14, 1634 and made a number of changes in the government.[3] Thomas Dudley was chosen governor and Roger Ludlow deputy-governor. Ludlow evidently had changed his mind about returning to England. A large part of the power previously exercised by the magistrates was

[1] *Mass. Col. Rec.*, vol. i, pp. 86, 101, 104, 106, 110.

[2] Winthrop (Savage), vol. i, pp. 152-3.

[3] *Mass. Col. Rec.*, vol. i, pp. 116-21; Winthrop (Savage), vol. i, pp. 157-8.

swept away at a single stroke. It was declared that the General Court alone had power to choose and admit freemen, to make and establish laws, to elect and appoint the principal officers and mark out their duties and powers, and to remove them upon misdemeanor. In addition to this it was asserted that none but the General Court could raise moneys and taxes and dispose of lands, *viz.*, give and confirm proprieties. All former orders concerning swine were repealed, and the provision was made that the towns should make such orders upon this subject as they judged best for themselves, and that if the swine of one town should come within the limits of another their owner would be liable to the orders of that town.[1] Another thrust was made at the magistrates in that some of them were questioned for certain errors in their government, and a number of fines were imposed upon them, but remitted before the Court adjourned.[2] As regarded the General Court itself, it was decided that there should be four sessions held each year, summoned by the governor and not dissolved without the consent of the major part of the Court. The freemen of the plantations were authorized to choose two or three of each town, who were to act for all except in the election of magistrates and other officers, in which each freemen was to give his own voice.[3]

The number of deputies present at this meeting was twenty-four,[4] three from each of the following towns: Newtown, Watertown, Charlestown, Boston, Roxbury, Dorchester, Saugus and Salem.[5] Three deputies were

[1] *Mass. Col. Rec.*, vol. i, p. 119.

[2] Winthrop (Savage), vol. i, p. 158.

[3] *Mass. Col. Rec.*, vol. i, pp. 118–9.

[4] *Ibid.*, vol. i, pp. 116–7.

[5] Palfrey, vol. i, p. 372, note.

returned by each town for several years; but because the number had greatly increased with the addition of new plantations, the General Court, March 13, 1638, thought best to reduce all towns to two deputies, in order to ease both the country and the Court.[1] Many of the towns, however, were much displeased with this arrangement, and with their deputies for voting in favor of it, since it was thought that the measure was only a scheme of the magistrates to extend their own power. At the next session, held May 22, 1639, it was proposed, therefore, that the towns be restored their former representation; but after a long debate and a thorough consideration of the reasons for the reduction, the question was put to a vote and the law was sustained.[2] This was the final arrangement as to the maximum number of representatives to be returned by the several towns, although the expediency of their sending only one was discussed later.[3] But it was referred to the various towns to decide whether they should send one or two,[4] and the result was a provision permitting the towns to send either one or two at their own pleasure.[5]

At the beginning of the session in 1634, a sermon was preached by Rev. John Cotton in which the doctrine was laid down that a magistrate should not be turned into the condition of a private man without just cause and a public trial, any more than the magistrates should turn a private man out of his freehold without like public trial. This question being raised in Court, the opinion of the other ministers was asked, but the whole affair

[1] *Mass. Col. Rec.*, vol. i, p. 254.

[2] Winthrop (Savage), vol. i, p. 361.

[3] *Mass. Col. Rec.*, vol. ii, p. 3.

[4] *Ibid.*, vol. ii, p. 217. [5] *Ibid*,, vol. ii, p. 231.

was finally postponed to a future time for discussion. In that Court, at least, no action was taken in opposition to the principle, since all the old assistants were rechosen.[1] But at the court of elections, held May 6, 1635, there was a sad departure from Cotton's doctrine. Aside from electing a new governor and deputy-governor, both Ludlow and Endicott were dropped from the magistracy.[2]

The popular enthusiasm seems to have cooled a little during the next few months, for at the General Court, held March 3, 1635, action was taken which was adverse to the former democratic tendencies. It was ordered that the next General Court should elect a certain number of magistrates for the term of their lives, as a standing council. These members were not to be removed except upon conviction of crime, insufficiency, or for some other weighty cause. The governor was always to be president of this council. Thus organized, it was to have such powers as the General Court should at any time see fit to bestow upon it.[3] The reason given at the time for this act was that, according to the word of God, the principal magistrates ought to be for life,[4] but the real purpose was probably to tempt to the colony some of the leading men of England.[5]

This measure was actually carried out, in part, at the next General Court, held May 25, 1636, when two of the members of the life council were chosen.[6] But it was not long until jealousy arose on the part of some of

[1] Winthrop (Savage), vol. i, p. 157. [2] *Ibid.*, vol. i, p. 188.

[3] *Mass. Col. Rec.*, vol. i, p. 167.

[4] Winthrop (Savage), vol. i, pp. 119-20.

[5] Hutchinson, vol. i, pp. 490-501.

[6] *Mass. Col. Rec.*, vol. i, p. 174; Winthrop (Savage), vol. i, pp. 119-20.

the deputies; and an order, passed June 6, 1639, virtually discontinued the life council, since it provided that all the magistrates were to be elected in the usual way.[1] The phrase "usual way" probably designated the democratic principle rather than the method of putting that principle into practice. The mode of electing the various officers had not yet become well established. During the first few years, the governor was elected by show of hands; but on May 14, 1634, Dudley was chosen by papers;[2] and in 1635 the governor and deputy-governor were elected by papers on which their names were written, but the assistants were chosen by papers without names. In voting for the latter, the governor proposed a name to the people, then they all went out and came in at one door and every man put a paper into a hat. Those who gave their vote for the person named put in a paper with some figures or scroll on it, the others threw in a blank.[3] At the General Court, held September 3, 1636, it was provided that the deputies should be elected thereafter by papers, as the governor was chosen;[4] also the franchise was defined in declaring that none but freemen should have a vote in any town relative to weighty matters or affairs, such as receiving inhabitants and laying out lots.[5] The qualifications of freemen will be noted later.

A few years later, a change was made in the manner of electing magistrates. This was brought about by an order of September 7, 1643, which provided that for the

[1] *Mass. Col. Rec.*, vol. i, p. 264; Winthrop (Savage), vol. i, pp. 363-4; Hubbard, p. 244.

[2] Winthrop (Savage), vol. i, p. 157.

[3] *Ibid.*, vol. i, p. 190.

[4] *Mass. Col. Rec.*, vol. i, p. 157.

[5] *Ibid.*, vol. i, p. 161.

yearly choice of assistants, in place of papers, the freemen should use Indian beans, the white signifying votes in favor of and the black votes against the candidate.[1] This provision was adopted in the revision of 1660[2] and also re-enacted in that of 1672,[3] with the change that Indian corn and beans should be used, the corn for votes in favor of and the beans for votes against the nominee. It was also added that if any freeman put in more than one Indian corn or bean for the choice or refusal of a public officer, he should forfeit for such offense ten pounds, and if any man who was not free, or had not the liberty of voting, put in a vote, he was to forfeit the same amount.

At first all the freemen were accustomed to assemble for the election of officers, but this was as difficult as it was to attend the other meetings of the General Court. As the population extended over a wider territory, it became both inconvenient and dangerous for the freemen of the more remote settlements to leave their homes. In addition to this, there was often a scarcity of food in the places where they met. In consequence of these facts, it was ordered, March 3, 1635, that the next General Court should be held at Boston, and that the freemen of Ipswich, Newberry, Salem, Saugus, Waymouth and Hingham might vote by proxy.[4] By order of March 9, 1636, it was provided that all the freemen might send their votes by proxy to the General Court to be held the following May. The manner in which this should be done was also prescribed. The chosen depu-

[1] *Mass. Col. Rec.*, vol. ii, p. 42.

[2] *Laws*, 1660-72 (ed. by Whitmore, Boston, 1889), p. 149.

[3] *Laws*, 1672-86 (ed. by Whitmore, Boston, 1887), p. 47.

[4] *Mass. Col. Rec.*, vol. i, p. 166; Winthrop (Savage), vol. i, p. 220.

ties were to assemble the freemen of their respective towns and then to take the votes of such as wished to send by proxy for each magistrate. These votes were to be sealed up and carried to the General Court along with a list of the names of the freemen who sent them.[1]

At first the General Court assembled at the summons of the governor, but it was declared, November 5, 1639, that thereafter upon the day appointed by the patent for the election of officers, which day was the last Wednesday of Easter term, the freemen, either in person or by proxy, should assemble without summons. They were also to send their deputies with full power to make laws and transact business. No magistrate or deputy could depart or be discharged from this session, without the consent of the major part of the Court, under the penalty of one hundred pounds.[2]

In 1634, as already stated, the number of General Courts to be held annually was raised to four. But as time advanced, it was found that so many sessions were not necessary. A law was passed, therefore, March 3, 1635, reducing the number to two, one to be held in May, for elections and other affairs, and the other on the first Wednesday in October, for making laws and transacting other public business. But the governor could call a special session at any time upon urgent occasion. It was further provided that no law, order or sentence should pass as an act of the Court without the assent of the greater number of the magistrates as well as that of the greater number of the deputies. But in case of a disagreement, and if either party should wish to carry the question further, a committee was to be chosen, half from each branch, and this committee was

[1] *Mass. Col. Rec.*, vol. i, p. 188.

[2] *Ibid.*, vol. i, p. 277.

to select an umpire who, together with the committee, might decide the question.[1]

Until 1643, the magistrates and deputies sat together, but before this time various disputes had arisen between them. One of these appeared as early as September 4, 1634, in the General Court held at Newtown. The question of Mr. Hooker's removal came up and was debated several days.[2] Many reasons were given both pro and con, and as the Court was divided, it was put to a vote. The governor and two assistants were for it, but the deputy and all the rest of the assistants, except the secretary who did not vote, were against it. No record was entered, since there were not six assistants in the vote as the patent required. From this affair resulted the question of the negative voice of the assistants. Some thought that the magistrates should not have such power, but others held that it was necessary to balance the greater number of deputies. Finally everything came to a deadlock, and it was agreed that a day of humiliation and prayer should be kept. This was done on the 18th, and on the 24th the Court met again. Before proceeding to business, Mr. Cotton preached and explained the nature or strength of the magistracy, the ministry, and the people; the strength of the magistracy was said to be their authority; that of the people, their liberty; and that of the ministry, their purity. He showed how all of these had a negative voice, and yet how the ultimate resolution ought to be in the whole body of the people, with answer to all objections and a declaration of the people's duty and right to maintain their true liberty against any unjust violence. This

[1] *Mass. Col. Rec.*, vol. i, pp. 169-70.

[2] Hutchinson, vol. i, p. 44.

doctrine gave great satisfaction, and the remainder of the session passed smoothly. Although not every one was satisfied with the negative voice of the magistrates, yet the matter was not brought up again during that Court.[1]

The question, however, was not settled. It was raised from time to time during the next few years, until the so-called "sow business" came up, which finally resulted in a division of the General Court into two houses.[2] This was accomplished by an order of March 4, 1643, which provided that the magistrates should sit and transact business by themselves. They were to draw up bills, and present such as they passed to the deputies for assent or rejection. In like manner the deputies were to present their measures to the magistrates for consideration. All bills passed thus by the majority of each body were to be laws. Such orders were to be engrossed and read deliberately the last day of the Court, when full assent was to be given.[3] Thus the negative voice of the magistrates was not taken away but duplicated in the lower house.[4]

The establishment of a bicameral legislature made necessary the office of speaker in the lower house, and at the next session of the General Court, May 30, 1644, William Hawthorn was chosen for that place. A number of other officers whom the deputies found necessary in their separate organization were elected at the same time.[5]

The governor, of course, still presided over the upper house, but he had no veto, and in fact he possessed

[1] Winthrop (Savage), vol. i, pp. 167–9.

[2] *Ibid.*, vol. ii, pp. 83–6, 139–44.

[3] *Mass. Col. Rec.*, vol. ii, pp. 58–59.

[4] Palfrey, vol. i, pp. 616–623.

[5] *Mass. Col. Rec.*, vol. iii, p. 2.

little more legislative authority than an ordinary magistrate. Before the separation of the houses, he had presided at the General Court and had put questions to vote, but if he refused to propose any question some one else would put it for him. A situation of this kind arose at the General Court held March 9, 1636. There was a dispute between Boston and some of the other towns over the Wheelright affair, and as a result a motion was made to hold the next session at Newtown. But Governor Vane refused to put the question to a vote. The deputy-governor excused himself because he resided in Boston. Then Endicott assumed the authority and put the motion, which was carried.[1] According to this decision the Court met at Newtown, May 17, 1637. As soon as it had assembled, which was about one o'clock, a petition from Boston was presented. The governor undertook to read it, but was opposed by the deputy, on the ground that the court had assembled for election, after which the petition might be heard. The governor and his party, however, would not proceed with the election unless the petition was read. Then it was moved by the deputy that the people divide themselves and the greater part carry the point. In this way it was found that by far the greater number was for election. But as the governor and his side would not yield, the deputy-governor took the initiative, and they proceeded with the elections.[2] The governor's power, however, was increased to a certain extent by Liberty 71, adopted in 1641. By this provision, which is also contained in the revisions of 1660[3] and 1672,[4] he was given a casting

[1] Winthrop (Savage), vol. i, pp. 258–9; *Mass. Col. Rec.*, vol. i, p. 101.

[2] Winthrop (Savage), vol. i, pp. 261–2.

[3] *Laws*, 1660–72, pp. 49, 143. [4] *Laws*, 1672–86, p. 35.

voice in case of a tie, both in the court of assistants and in the General Assembly. But an equal power was granted to the president or moderator of all civil courts or assemblies. This, of course, applied to the speaker of the lower house as well as to the governor in the upper house.

The adjustment of the two branches of the legislature, one to the other, took place gradually. At the General Court held October 18, 1648, it was ordered that, as there was a secretary among the magistrates, there should be a clerk in the lower house chosen by the deputies.[1] All bills, laws and petitions last concluded among the magistrates were to remain with the governor until the latter part of the session, and those last assented to by the deputies were to remain with the speaker until the same time, when the whole Court, or a committee of magistrates and deputies, was to meet together, to consider what laws had been passed. At this meeting the secretary and clerk were to be present, and by their journals call for such bills as passed either house. Such as should appear to have passed both the magistrates and deputies were to be delivered to the secretary to record, which he was to do within one month after each session.[2]

A great deal of inconvenience was incurred by reserving bills till the end of the session, and, apart from this, it was found desirable to know as soon as possible when a measure had passed both houses. An order of May 22, 1650, provided, therefore, that the clerk of the deputies should send up to the secretary such bills as had passed both houses, and last the lower house, and, in

[1] This marks the beginning of separate journals.

[2] *Mass. Col. Rec.*, vol. ii, p. 259.

like manner, that the secretary should send down to the clerk the measures last concluded by the assistants.[1] On the 18th of the following October an interpretation was placed upon the term majority. It seems that there had been some uncertainty in regard to this point. It was declared that the greater part of the magistrates and the greater part of the deputies should be interpreted to mean the greater number of those that were present and voted.[2]

But there was still a great defect in the legislative system, in that there was no rule providing for sufficient deliberation upon proposed measures. In order to remedy this, an act of May 6, 1657, after referring to the procedure of the Parliament of England in law making, declared that all measures, except transient acts, should be read and thoroughly considered on three different days. If they then received the approval and consent of the major part of the magistrates and deputies, they were to be of force.[3]

The above provision marks the extent, except in a few minor matters, of the development of the legislative department under the old charter. Not all the inhabitants, however, had a part in the government. The qualification of freemen had been fixed shortly after the transfer of the charter to America. But the question came up again, May 31, 1660, and the General Court declared that no man should be admitted to the freedom of the body politic except he were a member of some church of Christ and in full communion. This was avowed to be the meaning of the ancient law of 1631.[4] A modification

[1] *Mass. Col. Rec.*, vol. iv, pt. i, p. 3.

[2] *Ibid.*, vol. iv, pt. i, p. 35.

[3] *Ibid.*, vol. iv, pt. i, p. 292.

[4] *Ibid.*, vol. iv, pt. i, p. 420.

of this requirement, however, soon took place. To comply with a demand made by the king, in a letter dated June 28, 1662, the General Court held August 3, 1664, repealed the church membership requirement and substituted for it that of an upright character and orthodox belief in religion.[1]

During the next twenty years the legislative system underwent very little change. This period, however, witnessed the long struggle with the crown which finally resulted in the overthrow of the old colonial government. In June, 1683, Attorney-General Thomas Johnes filed an information in the nature of a writ of *quo warranto*.[2] This having failed, the process of *scire facias* was resorted to, and the final decree abrogating the charter was entered October 13, 1684.[3] But the Rose frigate, bearing the commission of Dudley, did not arrive at Boston until May 15, 1686.[4] On the 20th the General Court held a meeting; the establishment of the new government was proclaimed; and the Court adjourned till the second Wednesday in October. The government under the first charter was at an end.[5]

THE JUDICIAL SYSTEM

As already stated, the court of assistants exercised both legislative and judicial power until May 14, 1634. Until that time the General Assembly had been little

[1] *Mass. Col. Rec.*, vol. iv, pt. ii, p. 118.

[2] *Calender of State Papers. Col. Ser.* 1681-5, p. 451; Osgood, vol. iii, p. 331.

[3] *Calender of State Papers, Col. Ser.* 1681-5, p. 706; Osgood, vol. iii, p. 333.

[4] Sewall's Diary, vol. i, p. 137, says May 14th; Hutchinson, vol. i, p. 341; *Nar. and Crit. Hist.*, vol. iii, p. 321.

[5] Sewall's Diary, vol. i, pp. 138-40; *Mass. Col. Rec.*, vol. v, p. 517.

more than a court of elections.[1] With the assumption of legislative power by the General Court, the assistants tended to become a judicial body. But it was not long until specific provision was made for the administration of justice. This was done by an order passed March 3, 1635.[2] As already noted, there were to be, thereafter, two sessions of the General Court a year, with power lodged in the hands of the governor to call special sessions. In regard to the court of assistants, it was provided that there should be four great quarter courts, kept yearly at Boston by the governor and the rest of the magistrates. The time of holding the sessions was to be the first Tuesday in June, September, December, and March, and, to avoid conflict, the inferior courts were to meet the last Tuesday in the same months.

By the same act, provision was made for local courts. The towns were placed in four groups and the sessions were to be held every quarter at Ipswich, Salem, Newtown and Boston. Each of these courts was to be kept by such magistrates as dwelt in or near the place of meeting, and by such other persons as were, from time to time, appointed by the General Court. No court was to be held without one magistrate, but none of the magistrates who would attend were to be excluded. The General Court, however, was to designate the special magistrates for each court and also to choose from a list submitted by the towns a certain number of associates to sit with the magistrates, so that each court, counting the magistrates, should have five in all. Thus constituted, these local courts wese to try all civil causes, where the amount in controversy did not exceed ten

[1] Noble, *Pub. Mass. Col. Soc.*, vol. iii, p. 51.

[2] *Mass. Col. Rec.*, vol. i, pp. 169–70.

pounds, and all criminal causes not extending to life, limb or banishment. But if any person found himself grieved with a sentence he could appeal to the next great quarter court, on the condition "that hee putt in sufficient caution to present his appeale with effect & to abide the decision of the magistrates." The magistrates, however, were to see that those who brought appeals without just cause should be exemplarily punished.

All actions were to be tried at the court to which the defendant belonged. But all offenders that should be in the prison at Boston, when any court was held there, were to be tried at that court, unless reserved in the warrant of commitment to the great quarter court. Furthermore, it was made lawful for the governor, deputy-governor, or any two magistrates, upon special and urgent occasion, to appoint courts to be held on other days than those designated in the act.

In the above system, the General Court was of the first in importance. In discussing its power, it is necessary to go back to the declaration of May 14, 1634. This order avowed that the General Court had exclusive authority in certain named matters. This power was re-declared and extended in a number of subsequent acts, especially in that of November 13, 1644, which was passed in approval of the answer of the elders. Here it was affirmed that the General Court was the chief civil authority of the commonwealth and could act in all things belonging to it by virtue of such power. One of the powers especially mentioned was the judicial.[1] The various declarations were re-enacted in the revision of 1660,[2] and finally placed in that of 1672. The wording in the latter is as follows:

[1] *Mass. Col. Rec.*, vol. ii, p. 95. [2] *Laws*, 1660–72, pp. 141–2.

It is hereby declared that the General Court consisting of Magistrates and Deputies, is the chief Civil power of this commonwealth; which only hath power to Raise Money and Taxes upon the whole country, and dispose of Lands, viz., to Give and confirm Properties appertaining to and immediately derived from the country; and may Act in all affairs of this commonwealth according to such Power, both in matters of council, making of Laws, and matters of Judicature, by Impeaching and Sentencing any person or persons according to Law, and by receiving and hearing any complaints orderly presented against any person or court.[1]

Therefore, while the court of assistants was created by the charter, the number and times of its sessions and the extent of its jurisdiction could be governed by legislation. All courts inferior to that of the assistants were in every sense the creatures of statute.

The General Court itself would not proceed to judgment in any cause, civil or criminal, before the deputies had taken a solemn oath.[2] If the magistrates and deputies differed, the case was to be determined by the major vote of the whole Court met together.[3] From its decision there was no appeal.[4] Although the General Court had power to hear any case in first instance, it gradually became a court of appeals, and that for the most important matters only. June 14, 1642, it was declared that the General Court was to help only in cases where the party could get no relief in a lower court. Much time, the court complained, had been taken up in hearing and deciding particular cases between party and party which more properly belonged to an inferior court. Thereafter

[1] *Laws*, 1672–86, p. 34. [2] *Ibid.*

[3] *Laws*, 1660–72, p. 142; *Laws*, 1672–86, p. 35.

[4] *Plain Dealing* (Mass. Hist. Colls., 3rd Ser., vol. iii), p. 84. References are to this publication unless otherwise stated.

such causes were to be tried first in some lower court, and, if the losing party had any new evidence or other new matter to plead, he was to move a new trial in the same court upon a bill of review. If justice were not done him on that trial, he could then come to the General Court for relief.[1]

Provision was soon made for the manner in which appeals should be brought. This was done by order of May 2, 1649, which provided that all appeals lawfully obtained were to be accounted in the nature of a writ of error and, thereupon, all further proceedings in judgment and execution suspended.[2] This measure was misunderstood, since it was thought that appeal by writ of error revoked the whole judgment of the former court. In consequence of this defect, an act was passed May 3, 1654, which declared that in all cases of appeal the court appealed to should judge the cause according to the former evidence, and no other, but might rectify what was found amiss therein. When it was found that the judgment was in accordance with the evidence and with the law, the decree was not to be revoked, but the damages might be abated or increased to meet the demands of justice. No court was to transfer cases coming before it to the General Court, but if in doubt a court might suspend judgment and bring a statement of the case to the General Court, leaving out the names of the parties. The solution thus obtained was to be followed in disposing of that case at its next session.[3]

At first the General Court took cognizance of all cases both civil and criminal in which the bench and jury dis-

[1] *Mass. Col. Rec.*, vol. ii, p, 16; *Laws*, 1660–72, p. 197; *ibid.*, 1672–86, p. 152.

[2] *Mass. Col. Rec.*, vol. ii, p. 279.

[3] *Ibid.*, vol. iv. pt. i, p. 184.

agreed.[1] An order of May 3, 1654, set aside a day in that session for hearing such cases;[2] and on October 14, 1656, the method by which civil cases should be transferred from the county to the General Court was prescribed.[3] But by the revisions of 1660[4] and 1672[5] such civil cases from the county courts were to be brought before the court of assistants.[6] If in the court of assistants, however, two out of five, or three out of seven, or a like proportion of the magistrates dissented from the opinion of the court, in any capital offense, it was within the liberty of the party to appeal to the next General Court.[7]

Out of court, the governor and deputy-governor, agreeing together, or any three assistants by unanimous assent, could reprieve a condemned malefactor till the next court of assistants or General Court. But the General Court alone had power to pardon such a person.[8]

Next in importance to the General Court was the court of assistants. As already seen, according to the order of 1635[9] there were to be four sessions, but by order of

[1] Case of Mrs. Hibbins, *Mass. Col. Rec.*, vol. iv, pt. i, p. 269. Way *v.* Purchase, *Mass. Col. Rec.*, vol. iv, pt. i, p. 334.

[2] *Mass. Col. Rec.*, vol. iv. pt. i, p. 186.

[3] *Ibid.*, vol. iv, pt. i, p. 280.

[4] *Laws*, 1660–72, pp. 47–8.

[5] *Laws*, 1672–86, p. 87.

[6] There was no provision in these revisions for the transfer of criminal cases from the county court to either the General Court or court of assistants in case of disagreement between bench and jury, and the transfer in civil cases was discontinued by order of May 15, 1672. *Mass. Col. Rec.*, vol. iv, pt. ii, pp. 508–9.

[7] *Laws*, 1660–72, p. 122; *Laws*, 1672–86, p. 3. Also if the bench and jury disagreed in a capital offense it could be taken to the General Court. Case of Saucers, *Mass. Col. Rec.*, vol. iv, pt. i, p. 213.

[8] Liberty, 72; *Laws*, 1672–86, p. 35.

[9] *Plain Dealing*, p. 83.

October 17, 1649, the number was reduced to two, one in March and the other in September.[1] The governor, however, or, in his absence, the deputy-governor, could call a court for the trial of any person in a capital case, so that justice might not be delayed.[2] This arrangement, as is shown by the later statutes, was final.[3]

Although the quorum of the court of assistants was fixed by the charter, yet the General Court departed from the rule in passing an order, November 13, 1644, which declared that five magistrates would be sufficient to constitute a valid court the next session. The reasons given for this order were the distance some of the assistants had to come, the condition of the roads at that time of year and the fact that most of the important business had already been transacted.[4] The provision, however, was a special one and affected only the following session.

As to the original jurisdiction of the court of assistants, no direct declaration was at first made. It may be concluded, however, that all original jurisdiction not granted to county courts was left to the General Court and court of assistants. Thomas Lechford makes no distinction between these two courts. He says:

> In the general court, or great quarter courts, before the Civill Magistrates, are tryed all actions and causes civill and criminall and also Ecclesiastical, especially touching non-members. And they themselves say, that in the general and quarter Courts, they have the power of Parliament, Kings Bench, Common Pleas, Chancery, High Commission, and Star Chamber, and all other Courts of England, and in divers

[1] Noble, *Pub. Mass. Col. Soc.*, vol. iii, p. 52.

[2] *Mass. Col. Rec.*, vol. ii, p. 286.

[3] *Laws*, 1660–72, p. 143; *Laws*, 1672–86, p. 36.

[4] *Mass. Col. Rec.*, vol. ii, p. 85.

cases have exercised that power upon the King's Subjects there as is not difficult to prove. They have put to death, banished, fined men, cut off men's ears, whipped, imprisoned men, and all these for Ecclesiasticall and Civill offenses, and without sufficient record.

He adds, however: "From the petie quarter Courts, or other court, the parties may appeale to the great quarter Courts, from thence to the general court from which there is no appeal, they say: Notwithstanding, I presume their Patent doth reserve and provide for Appeals, in some cases, to the Kings Majesty."[1] But after the time of which Lechford wrote, the General Court, as already shown, became only an appellate court in civil causes. That it also became only an appellate court in criminal matters will appear when the development of the original jurisdiction of the court of assistants is noted.

To remove the burden of concurrent jurisdiction with lower courts, it was ordered, May 2, 1649, that the court of assistants should take cognizance of no case or action tryable in any county court, unless it were by way of appeal.[2] Then, by a provision contained in the revision of 1660[3] and continued in that of 1672,[4] the jurisdiction of the court of assistants was set forth. It was to extend only to actions of appeal from inferior courts, all causes of divorce,[5] all capital and criminal causes extending to life, limb, or banishment. Aside from this an order, passed January 6, 1673, provided that all ad-

[1] *Plain Dealing*, pp. 83-4.
[2] *Mass. Col. Rec.*, vol. ii, p. 279.
[3] *Laws*, 1660-72, p. 143.
[4] *Laws*, 1672-86, p. 36.

[5] The Court of Assistants probably had jurisdiction of divorce cases by the code of 1649. Whitmore, *Bibliog. Sketch*, p. 101, note. But the General Court could take cognizance of divorce cases in first instance on petition.

miralty cases should be heard and determined by the court of assistants. In such cases the court was to sit without a jury, unless it should see good reason to do otherwise. This act, however, was not to be interpreted to obstruct the just pleas of mariners or merchants in other courts.[1]

Besides exercising the ordinary appellate jurisdiction, the court of assistants at first heard civil cases from the county courts in which the court and jury failed to agree. The same evidence was used as recorded in the county court, but both parties were at liberty to make new pleas or bring in new evidence before the bench and jury. If the plaintiff failed to prosecute the case, the decision was to be for the defendant.[2] But this provision was repealed by an act of May 15, 1672, and the remedy of attaint of juries was put in its place.[3]

In order to relieve the court of assistants, it was ordered, September 9, 1639, that the magistrates who resided in or near Boston, or any five, four or three of them, the governor or deputy included, should assemble the fifth day of the eighth, eleventh, second and fifth months, and hear all civil causes, not exceeding twenty pounds, and all criminal matters, not extending to life, limb, or banishment. An appeal lay from this special court to that of the assistants.[4] Just what became of this court is not clear. Lechford seems to have confounded it with the county court of Boston when he says: "In the lesser quarter courts are tryed, in some,

[1] *Mass. Col. Rec.*, vol. iv, pt. ii, p. 575.

[2] *Laws*, 1660–72, pp. 167–8; *Laws*, 1672–86, p. 87.

[3] *Mass. Col. Rec.*, vol. iv, pt. ii, pp. 508–9; *Laws*, 1672–86, p. 201.

[4] *Mass. Col. Rec.*, vol. i, p. 276; Noble, *Pub. Mass. Col. Soc.*, vol. iii, p. 52.

actions under ten pounds, in Boston, under twenty, and all criminal causes not touching life or member."[1] The object was to thrust this court between the assistants and the county courts, and it appears that as soon as the need of it passed away the court was discontinued. At any rate, no provision was made in later revisions for such a court.

Directly beneath the court of assistants were the county or shire courts. Their number and jurisdiction according to the Act of 1635, which created them, have already been discussed. Lechford, in speaking of them, says: "There are other petie courts, one every quarter, at Boston, Salem and Ipswich, with their severall jurisdictions."[2] The name of Cambridge, given May 2, 1638, to the town before known as Newtown,[3] is omitted. This is doubtless due to inaccuracy of description and does not indicate the suspension of the court at that place.

As already noted, there was to be a court every quarter in each of the four designated towns. But in order to relieve the colony of all unnecessary travel and expense, it was provided, June 2, 1641, that there should be four quarter courts kept yearly by the magistrates of Ipswich and Salem, with such others as were joined in commission with them by the General Court. But this was not to hinder other magistrates from assisting. These courts were to be held the first and third quarter at Ipswich, the second and fourth at Salem. The magistrates of both towns were to attend all the courts, but jurymen were not to be warned (*i. e.*, summoned) from either place to the other. To either town a grand jury

[1] *Plain Dealing*, p. 84.

[2] *Ibid.*, p. 83.

[3] *Mass, Col. Rec.*, vol. i, p. 228.

was to be summoned once a year. Salsbury and Hampton were joined to the jurisdiction of Ipswich, and each of them was to send yearly a grand juryman thither.[1]

The grouping of the towns into quarter-court jurisdictions and the division of the military force into regiments, assigned to certain districts, which took place December 13, 1636,[2] formed the basis for counties or shires.[3] Four of these were established May 10, 1643, and given the English names of Essex, Middlesex, Suffolk, and Norfolk.[4] At first Norfolk had no county court. As stated above, Salsbury and Hampton were joined to Ipswich; but in March, 1647, a court was established in Norfolk, to be held at Salsbury by the same magistrates that sat at Dover.[5] Several new counties were added later. According to the revisions of 1660[6] and 1672,[7] there were: Suffolk, with four courts a year; Norfolk, with two; Essex, with four; Piscataqua, with one; Middlesex, with four; Yorkshire, with one; and Hampshire, with two. October 7, 1674, Devonshire was added, with one court a year.[8]

Certain magistrates and associates were appointed, May 25, 1636, for each of the county courts, and it was declared at the same time that court could be held by three of the persons appointed, provided one were a magistrate. In the place of judicature the king's arms were to be erected.[9] That two associates with one magistrate should constitute a quorum was the final

[1] *Mass. Col. Rec.*, vol. i, p. 325.
[2] *Ibid.*, vol. i, pp. 186-7.
[3] Palfrey, vol. i, p. 617.
[4] *Mass. Col. Rec.*, vol. ii, p. 38.
[5] *Ibid.*, vol. ii, p. 227.
[6] *Laws*, 1660-72, pp. 143-4.
[7] *Laws*, 1672-86, p. 37.
[8] *Mass. Col. Rec.*, vol. v, pp. 16-7; *Laws*, 1672-86, p. 218.
[9] *Mass. Col. Rec.*, vol. i, p. 175.

arrangement, according to the revisions of 1660[1] and 1672.[2] The associates, although appointed by the General Court, were to be nominated by the freemen of the county,[3] and by act of May 27, 1674, these nominations were to be made at the same time as those for magistrates.[4]

As there had been a special court in Boston to relieve the court of assistants, so there was at the same place a special court to relieve the county court. This court was created by act of October 14, 1651, which provided that seven freemen resident in Boston should be chosen annually by the freemen and authorized by the court of assistants to be commissioners of judicature. Five of the seven were to constitute a quorum, or three with one magistrate could keep a court. At first their territorial jurisdiction was limited to the neck of land on which the town was situated and to Noodles Island,[5] but was extended by act of October 7, 1674, to the whole limits of Boston.[6]

By the law of 1635 the county courts had power to try all civil causes, where the amount in controversy did not exceed ten pounds, and all criminal causes not extending to life, limb, or banishment.[7] An exception was made to this in the act of 1641, relating to the quarter courts of Ipswich and Salem.[8] These courts were to have the same power, both in civil and criminal causes, as the court of assistants at Boston, excepting trials for

[1] *Laws*, 1660–72, p. 148. [2] *Laws*, 1672–86, p. 36.

[3] *Laws*, 1660–72, p. 143; *Laws*, 1672–86, p. 36.

[4] *Mass. Col. Rec.*, vol. v, p. 4.

[5] *Mass. Col. Rec.*, vol. iv, pt. i, pp. 59–60; *Laws*, 1660–72, p. 133; *Laws*, 1672–86, pp. 21–2.

[6] *Mass. Col. Rec.*, vol. v, pp. 15–16; *Laws*, 1672–86, p. 217.

[7] *Mass. Col. Rec.*, vol. i, p. 169, [8] *Ibid.*, vol. i, p. 325.

life, limb, or banishment, which were wholly reserved to the Boston court. An appeal, however, could be taken to Boston, and any plaintiff that had an action of debt above one hundred pounds' principal was at liberty to try his cause in either of these courts or at Boston. This provision formed in large measure the basis for the jurisdiction of the county courts as established in the revisions of 1660[1] and 1672.[2] In these it was provided that the county courts should have power to try all causes, civil and criminal, not extending to life, limb, or banishment; the latter, with causes of divorce, were reserved to the court of assistants. The county courts were also to appoint clerks and other needful officers and to summon juries of inquest and trial from the towns; but no jurors were to be summoned from Ipswich to Salem or from Salem to Ipswich.[3]

To what petty matters the original jurisdiction of the county courts extended will appear later. It is sufficient to say here that it extended at first to all causes, but was limited later to causes above twenty shillings and, finally, to those above forty shillings.

Another exception to the general jurisdiction of the county courts was that of the commissioners at Boston. The territory over which this court was to exercise its power has already been noted. It could, within those limits, take cognizance of all civil actions not exceeding ten pounds, and in criminal causes it could exercise the same power as any magistrate, but could not impose fines of over forty shillings. From its decision an appeal lay to the court of assistants.[4]

[1] *Laws*, 1660-72, p. 143.

[2] *Laws*, 1672-86, p. 36.

[3] Hutchinson, vol. i, p. 450.

[4] *Laws*, 1660-72, p. 133; *Laws*, 1672-86, pp. 21-2; *Mass. Col. Rec.*, vol. iv, pt. i, pp. 59-60.

In addition to their general powers, the county courts had jurisdiction over a number of special matters, such as admitting church members to be freemen,[1] purging towns of heterodoxy,[2] appointing certain persons to look after bridges,[3] laying out highways, judging profaners of the Sabbath,[4] granting licenses,[5] settling paupers,[6] instructing the Indians[7] and exercising certain jurisdiction over them.[8]

May 2, 1649, it was ordered that no debt or action proper to the cognizance of any one magistrate or of any three commissioners, for trial of causes under forty shillings, should be entertained by a county court or court of assistants, except by appeal.[9] In case of defamation and battery, however, this rule did not apply.[10] But the county court might hear causes of defamation and battery in first instance. It had appellate jurisdiction in all matters tried by commissioners of small causes,[11] by single magistrates,[12] or by selectmen.[13]

For the protection of testamentary rights, it was provided, in the revision of 1672, that every will was to be probated in the next county court which should convene thirty days or more after the death of the party. In case any one should die intestate, the county court under whose jurisdiction the party had last resided was to have power to distribute the estate.[14] By an order of May 27, 1685, the magistrates of each county court were to have

[1] *Laws*, 1672–86, p. 38.
[2] *Ibid.*, p. 46.
[3] *Ibid.*, pp. 12, 64.
[4] *Ibid.*, pp. 133–4.
[5] *Mass. Col. Rec.*, vol. ii, p. 188.
[6] *Laws*, 1672–86, p. 123.
[7] *Mass. Col, Rec.*, vol. ii, p. 84.
[8] *Ibid.*, vol. ii, p. 188.
[9] *Ibid.*, vol. ii, p. 279.
[10] *Laws*, 1672–86, p. 21.
[11] *Ibid.*
[12] *Ibid.*, pp. 91–2.
[13] *Ibid.*, p. 148.
[14] *Ibid.*, pp. 157–8.

the same power as the ordinary in England to summon any executor or otherwise require him to present a sworn inventory of the property of the deceased. They were also to hear and determine all cases relating to wills and administrations, but, as in other matters, appeal lay to the court of assistants.[1] This measure was practically re-enacted by the order of October 14, 1685, with the addition that when matter of fact was controverted, either plaintiff or defendant might demand a jury.[2] The above act was repealed by an order of February 16, 1685, which provided that, whereas the magistrates or members of the county courts had always possessed power to receive and record all probates of wills and to grant administrations, each county court should have certain probate powers. But the powers named were very similar to those included in the previous acts. The authorization of a jury in question of fact and the liberty of appeal to the court of assistants were both retained.[3]

Below the county courts were the courts for the trial of small matters. Lechford says: "Every town, almost, hath a petie court for small debts and trespasses under twenty shillings."[4] These courts had been established about two years prior to the time of which Lechford wrote. This was accomplished by an order, passed September 6, 1638, which declared that any magistrate, in the town where he resided, might settle all causes in which the amount did not exceed twenty shillings. In towns where there was no magistrate, the General Court

[1] *Mass. Col. Rec.*, vol. v, pp. 478–9.

[2] *Ibid.*; vol. v, pp. 503–4; *Laws*, 1672–86, pp. 330–1.

[3] *Mass. Col. Rec.*, vol. v, pp. 508–9; *Laws*, 1672–86, pp. 333–4.

[4] *Plain Dealing*, p. 83.

was, from time to time, to appoint three men, two of whom should be a quorum.[1] But if any party found himself grieved by a decision, he could appeal to the next quarter court or court of assistants. If any person, however, brought such action to the assistants before he had endeavored to have it ended at home, he was to lose his action and pay the defendant's costs. If no appeal were put in on the day of the sentence, the magistrate or two chosen men were to grant execution.[2] Later, the jurisdiction of the small courts was extended from twenty to forty shillings, and, by order of November 11, 1647, the three commissioners were required to keep a record.[3]

Since the magistrates have been referred to at various times, a brief statement in regard to them will not be out of place. Magistrate was the term often applied to an assistant. According to the charter there were to be eighteen of them.[4] Later their number was raised to twenty; then it was reduced to fourteen, by the law of October 19, 1659;[5] and finally the old number of eighteen was restored, October 12, 1670.[6]

The order of 1638 was followed by the appointment of commissioners of small causes in various towns. It was further provided, by act of June 2, 1641, that, if the commissioners should at any time desire the help of one of the neighboring magistrates, the magistrate called upon should have authority to repair thither, whenever he should think fit, and aid the cause of justice by giving advice and administering oaths.[7]

[1] Hutchinson, vol. i, p. 450.

[2] *Mass. Col. Rec.*, vol. i, p. 239.

[3] *Ibid.*, vol. ii, p. 208.

[4] Poore, pt. i, p. 936.

[5] *Mass. Col. Rec.*, vol. iv, pt. i, p. 347.

[6] *Ibid.*, vol. iv, pt. ii, p. 468.

[7] *Ibid.*, vol. i, p. 327.

But there were various defects in the administration of justice by small courts. One of these was removed by act of October 7, 1646, which provided that the five or seven men in each town selected for prudential affairs should have power to determine causes in which the magistrate was interested and to grant execution for the collection of allowed damages.[1] Other imperfections were corrected and several minor additions made by provisions in the later revisions. The selectmen were to act in case the three commissioners were interested, just as they were to act in case the magistrate was interested. The magistrate was to proceed without a jury, a provision which probably referred to all the smaller courts, since the commissioners were appointed in towns where there was no magistrate, and since the selectmen acted when either of the former was interested.[2]

Other powers besides those already stated were given at various times to the selectmen. A few of these are worthy of note. By order of May 20, 1642, they were given authority to lay out private ways in their own towns and to exercise for a period of two years control over children in matters of industry, education and religion.[3] A law of August 30, 1653, required them to make orders for the repairing of certain fences and gave them power to enforce their orders by imposing upon delinquents[4] fines not exceeding twenty shillings. It was added, May 14, 1656, that they should apportion the spinning among the families of their towns, and make regulations for pasturing sheep;[5] and by order of May

[1] *Mass. Col. Rec.*, vol. ii, pp. 162-3; Hutchinson, vol. i, p. 451.

[2] *Laws*, 1660-72, pp. 132-3; *Laws*, 1672-86, pp. 20-1.

[3] *Mass. Col. Rec.*, vol. ii, pp. 4, 8, 9.

[4] *Ibid.*, vol. iv, pt. i, pp. 153-4. [5] *Ibid.*, vol. iv, pt. i, p. 256.

6, 1657, they were to regulate constables' watches.[1] Various other duties were imposed upon them in later revisions.[2]

For the adjudication of causes relative to strangers, there was, for a time, a separate system of courts and procedure. An arrangement had been made, by act of 1635, for special courts. But a measure of June 6, 1839, which had for its purpose the more speedy despatch of causes relative to strangers, established a special court for those who could not await the regular processes of justice. This court was to be held by the governor or deputy and two magistrates, and its jurisdiction extended to all causes between strangers or in which a stranger was a party. Trial was to be by jury, and all records were to be entered at the charge of the parties.[3] Provision was made for the stranger's court in the later revisions, with the addition that, in case the governor or deputy could not attend, the court could be held by three magistrates. Its jurisdiction was limited to causes, civil and criminal, triable in country courts. No appeal was provided. This was due, perhaps, to the fact that the purpose was to end cases as quickly as possible. Strangers, however, could enter actions against other strangers in the regular courts of the colony.[4]

The provision permitting causes between strangers to be brought in any court was passed June 21, 1650. This was in consequence of the fact that the special courts had been found very expensive for the strangers and inconvenient for the country.[5] But they were not discontinued

[1] *Mass. Col. Rec.*, vol. iv, pt. i, p. 293.

[2] *Cf.* Selectmen, in *Laws*, 1660–72, and in *Laws*, 1672–86.

[3] *Mass. Col. Rec.*, vol. i, p. 264.

[4] *Laws*, 1660–72, p. 144; *Laws*, 1672–86, pp. 37–8.

[5] *Mass. Col. Rec.*, vol. iv, pt. i, p. 20.

until October 8, 1672. The act which abolished them declared that a stranger might sue another stranger, or a stranger in immediate employ as mariner or merchant might sue an inhabitant, in any court of the colony which had cognizance of such matters. In case an inhabitant were sued outside his own county, the plaintiff had to give to the clerk of writs security for the payment of all extraordinary costs which the defendant would thus incur, and which, of course, the plaintiff would have to pay if he did not win the suit.[1]

Aside from the special courts mentioned above, there was a special probate court, which was created primarily in the interest of strangers. It was established by an act contained in the revisions of 1660 and 1672 and dated 1652. Any two magistrates, with the recorder or clerk of the county court, were empowered to probate wills, or to grant administration of the estate of any one dying intestate, in that county. But the recorder or clerk was to inform the rest of the magistrates at the next county court of such will probated or administration granted.[2] The reason assigned for this provision was that many strangers had died without having made a disposition of their estates, and frequently it was very difficult to preserve these estates until the next meeting of the county court.

Associated with the various courts were certain officers whose duties were either semi-judicial or executive. A law of December 10, 1641, stated that, although every magistrate had power to grant warrants, summonses and attachments, there should be a clerk of the writs, nominated by each town and allowed by the shire court. This

[1] *Mass. Col. Rec.*, vol. iv, pt. ii, p. 532; *Laws*, 1672–86, p. 207.

[2] *Laws*, 1660–72, p. 201; *Laws*, 1672–86, p. 158.

clerk was to grant summonses and attachments in all civil actions, upon the application of the plaintiff, and also summonses for witnesses. He could grant replevin, but was to require bond, with a sufficient security, for the prosecution of the suit.[1] As is shown by the later revisions the clerkship became a permanent office.[2]

The executive officer of the General Court was at first called the "beadle,"[3] but in 1634 he was given the title of "marshal."[4] Later he was known as "marshal general," while the executive officers of inferior courts were called "marshals."[5] Also the various towns annually elected constables, who not only acted as local police but also carried out court decrees.[6] In addition to these officers, there were clerks or recorders for the courts and keepers of the prisons. The above-named officers constituted the administrative machinery of justice.[7]

Such was the judicial system under the old charter, except that provision was made for the administration of military law. But before taking this up, mention should be made of the legislation which had for its purpose the purification of the courts thus far described. In 1643 an act was passed which prohibited a judge from exercizing authority in any civil case, involving a considerable amount, if either party were a near relative of his.[8] An order of 1649 forbade any one's asking counsel of a magistrate concerning a pending suit in which he was a party.[9]

[1] *Mass. Col. Rec.*, vol. i, pp. 344-5.

[2] *Laws*, 1660-72, p. 138; *Laws*, 1672-86, pp. 28-9.

[3] *Plain Dealing*, p. 85; *Mass. Col. Rec.*, vol. i, pp. 40, 74, 100.

[4] *Mass. Col. Rec.*, vol. i, p. 129.

[5] *Laws*, 1660-72, p. 173; *Laws*, 1672-86, p. 103.

[6] *Mass. Col. Rec.*, vol. i, p. 76; vol. iv, pt. i, pp. 324-27; *Laws*, 1660-72, pp. 139-40; *Laws*, 1672-86, pp. 31-2.

[7] *Laws*, 1660-72, pp. 138, 143, 196; *Laws*, 1672-86, pp. 28, 128.

[8] *Mass. Col. Rec.*, vol. ii, p. 39.

[9] *Ibid.*, vol. ii, p. 279.

But more important still was the law passed in 1653, which declared that no person, who had sat as judge or had voted on a cause in an inferior court, should have any vote in the superior court if the same cause should come before it on appeal.[1]

The administration of military law was provided for in the early days of the colony. By act of September 3, 1634, the governor and four of the assistants were constituted a military commission for one year.[2] March 4, 1634, the commission was extended till the end of the next General Court. It was also enlarged, and it received power to administer all military laws and, among other things, to pronounce even the death sentence.[3] This commission was extended from session to session[4] until October 28, 1636, when the military power was lodged in the hands of the standing council until the session in the following May.[5] April 18, 1637, it was confirmed in the hands of the council until further order should be taken.[6] This was apparently the final disposition of the power of court-martial. In the revisions of 1660 and 1672, the council had authority over military affairs, and, although nothing is said about the administration of military law, it is probable that such power was understood to be included. Such an assumption is the more reasonable in view of the fact that the court of assistants and the council were identical, except in a few minor points. It was in reality the same body acting in two different capacities.[7]

In addition to the military power of the council, cer-

[1] *Mass. Col. Rec.*, vol. iv, pt. i, p. 152.

[2] *Ibid.*, vol. i, p. 125.

[3] *Ibid.*, vol. i, p. 138.

[4] *Ibid.*, vol. i, pp. 161, 168.

[5] *Ibid.*, vol. i, p. 183.

[6] *Ibid.*, vol. i, p. 192.

[7] *Laws*, 1660–72, p. 141; *Laws*, 1672–86, p. 33–4.

tain officers were given authority to impose small penalties. At first the two officers of every trained band were authorized to punish delinquents. An order of November 11, 1647, declared that the three chief officers of each company, or any two of them, should have power to punish soldiers offending upon training day, at the time of military exercise, or upon any watch or ward. They could place the offender in the bilboes, subject him to other usual military punishment, or fine him not over twenty shillings, or they might turn him over to the constable to be brought before a magistrate, who could bind him over to the next court of the shire, if the case required, or commit him to prison.[1] This provision was continued in the revisions of 1660 and 1672 and was, therefore, a permanent arrangement in the first period.[2]

An attempt was made to break into the judicial system of the colony by establishing a royal court. July 23, 1664, Colonel Richard Nichols, George Cartwright, Sir Robert Carr and Samuel Maverick arrived in Boston. They had received a commission from the king for reducing the Dutch, visiting the colonies in New England, hearing and determining all matters of complaint, and settling the peace and security of the country. But after a stubborn resistance on the part of the freemen, the commissioners abandoned the task of establishing their power in Massachusetts.[3] The courts of the colony remained as described until a new government was organized under Dudley.

[1] *Mass. Col. Rec.*, vol. ii, p. 223.

[2] *Laws*, 1660–72, p. 177; *Laws*, 1672–86, p. 108.

[3] *Mass. Col. Rec.*, vol. iv, pt. ii, pp. 117–8, 203–4, 206–10, 279–80; Hutchinson, vol. i, pp. 230–1, 246–9; Oliver, *The Puritan Commonwealth* (Boston, 1856), ch. iv, pt. ii; Washburn, *Sketches of the Judicial History of Massachusetts* (Boston, 1840), pp. 35–6.

THE CHURCH

Although the colonists, when they left their mother country, professed great love and respect for the Church of England, they seemed to have had in mind the establishment of a church of their own. Higginson said that they did "not go to New England as Separatists from the Church of England, though" they could not "but separate from the corruptions in it; but" that they went "to practice the positive part of the Church reformation. and to propagate the Gospel in America."[1] The controversy between the Browns and the ministers after arriving at Salem throws some light upon what was meant by the "positive part of Church reformation." When Win throp and his company left for America, the next year, they were more emphatic still in the expression of their loyalty to the established church,[2] but on the voyage over Winthrop indicated in a sermon that they were engaged in an enterprise of more than ordinary significance.[3]

The churches established by the colonists pledged conformity to the word of God, not to the Church of England.[4] The manner in which churches were organized is described by Thomas Lechford. A number of Christians, allowed by the General Court to plant together, assembled on a fixed day and entered into a covenant with God and one another. Then they elected their own officers, consisting of a pastor, a teacher, elders, and deacons, if they had men enough fit to fill these places; if not, they filled

[1] Ellis, *The Puritan Age and Rule* (Boston and New York, 1888), p. 55.

[2] *The Company's Humble Request*, (Young, Chronicles), p. 296.

[3] *A Modell of Christian Charity*, (Mass. Hist. Coll., 3d series, vol. vii), pp. 45-46.

[4] Ellis, *Puritan Age*, p. 59.

as many as they could.[1] While these churches did not renounce their relation with the Church of England, yet they dispensed with "the liturgy, the read prayers, the responsive service, days of observance, other than the Sabbath, and the official relation of the minister."[2] In 1633 Winthrop wrote in his journal that certain enemies of the colony had petitioned the king and council against them, accusing them of intending rebellion, of having cast off their allegiance and of wholly separating from the church and laws of England. The members of the company who were in England were called before a committee of the council, but their answer pleased both the lords and his majesty. The defendants were dismissed and assured by some of the council that his majesty did not intend to impose the ceremonies of the Church of England upon the colonists, for it was considered that the freedom from such things attracted people thither.[3] The rejection of those forms, however, did finally make out of the colonial church a separate and distinct institution, and when the mother church presented itself for recognition about thirty-two years later, it was regarded as an unwelcome intruder.[4]

Throughout the whole period of the first charter, the church was closely connected with the state. As early as 1631 church membership was declared a requisite for admission to the freedom of the body politic.[5] This provision was re-enacted in 1660[6] and remained in force until 1664, when it was repealed and an obscure order put in

[1] *Plain Dealing*, pp. 63–4.

[2] Ellis, *Puritan Age*, p. 60.

[3] Winthrop (Savage), vol. i, pp. 122–3.

[4] *Mass. Col. Rec.*, vol. iv, pt. ii, pp. 192, 200, 212, 220.

[5] *Ibid.*, vol. i, p. 87. [6] *Ibid.*, vol. iv, pt. i, p. 420.

its place. But still the minister retained great power, for the applicant, if not a church member, was required, among other things, to present a certificate, under the hand of the minister or ministers of the place where he dwelt, to the effect that he was orthodox in religion and not vicious in his life.[1] This provision gave the minister power to exercise a wide discretion, and it is not likely that it greatly modified the basis of the franchise.

Since the church was the gateway to political privilege and power, it was necessary for the preservation of the state to keep the church pure and orthodox. But gradually diversity of opinion grew up in the churches; and even after the banishment of Mrs. Hutchison and Wheelwright and their followers, errors continued to thrive, and many of the ministers were in disaccord upon various points, such as infant baptism. In view of these facts, the General Court turned its attention to the question of church government. It declared, May 2, 1646, that it had power, by the word of God, to assemble the churches upon occasion of counsel, but that, since all the members of the churches were not satisfied on that point, it was thought expedient not to make use of such power, but to express a desire that all churches should send elders and other members to meet at Cambridge, in the following September. The purpose of this synod was to frame a form of goverment and discipline for the whole church organization.[2] With all its modesty, however, the General Court, October 27, 1647, took upon itself the authority to name certain persons who should prepare a

[1] *Mass. Col. Rec.*, vol. iv, pt. ii, p. 118; *Laws*, 1660–72, p. 229; *Laws*, 1672–86, p. 56.

[2] *Mass. Col. Rec.*, vol. ii, pp. 154–5; Winthrop (Savage), vol. ii, pp. 323–4.

brief form of confession of faith and present the same to the next session of the synod.[1]

At length, during August, 1648, the synod succeeded in drawing up a form of discipline.[2] This was referred by the General Court in 1649 to the various churches for consideration.[3] But since many of the churches were ignorant of the order and failed to act upon the propositions, the Court recommended the work of the Cambridge synod anew in the following year.[4] The churches sent in their objections, which were delivered to Rev. Mr. Cotton to be communicated to the elders, who should pass upon them in meeting assembled and present their advise to the next General Court.[5] This was done, and the General Court, October 14, 1651, gave its testimony to the book of discipline, declaring that "for the substance thereof it is that we have practiced and doe believe."[6] Thus the Church Platform received the sanction of law.

At a synod held in Boston, September 10, 1679, of which the Rev. Increase Mather was moderator, it was put to a vote, whether the assembly did approve of the Platform of Church Discipline, and the vote in the affirmative was unanimous. The following resolution was then passed:

A synod of the churches in the province of Massachusetts, being called by the honored General Court to convene at Boston, the 10th of September, 1679, having read and considered the Platform of Church Discipline, agreed upon by

[1] *Mass. Col. Rec.*, vol. ii, p. 200. The synod had already met twice and adjourned after a very brief session. Winthrop (Savage), vol. ii, pp. 328-32, 376; *The Cambridge and Saybrook Platforms of Church Discipline* (Boston, 1829), Hist. Pref., p. 6.

[2] Winthrop (Savage), vol ii, p. 403; *Platforms*, Hist. Pref., p. 6.

[3] *Mass. Col. Rec.*, vol. ii, p. 285.

[4] *Ibid.*, vol. iv, pt. i, p. 22.

[5] *Ibid.*, vol. iv, p. i, pp. 54-5.

[6] *Ibid.*, vol. iv, pt. i, p. 57.

the synod assembled at Cambridge, 1648, do unanimously approve of the said Platform, for the substance of it, desiring that the churches may continue steadfast in the order of the gospel according to what is therein declared from the word of God.[1]

At a second session the 12th of the following May, the synod adopted a confession of faith. The result of the synod was presented to the General Court, and the following order was passed, June 11, 1680:

This Court, having taken into serious consideration the requests which hath been presented by several of the reverend elders, in the name of the late synod, doe approve thereof, and accordingly order the confession of faith agreed upon at their second session, and the Platform of Discipline, consented unto by the synod at Cambridge, anno 1648, to be presented for the benefit of these churches in present and after time.[2]

The Cambridge Platform, therefore, became the permanent exposition of the position and power of the church, ratified by both church and state.[3]

According to the Cambridge Platform it was "unlawful for church officers to meddle with the sword of the magistrate" and "the magistrate to meddle with the work proper to church officers." But it was the "duty of the magistrate to take care of matters of religion." "Idolatry, blasphemy, heresy, venting corrupt and pernicious opinions, that destroy the foundation, open contempt of the word preached, profanation of the Lord's day, disturbing the peaceable administration and exercise of the worship and holy things of God, and the like" were "to be restrained and punished by civil authority."

[1] *Platforms*, Hist. Pref., p. 9. [2] *Mass. Col. Rec.*, vol. v, p. 287.

[3] *Platforms*, Hist. Pref., p. 12.

Also the magistrate was to use coercion in the case of a church that should withdraw from the communion of the other churches.[1] Thus there was to be a state church in Massachusetts, and no other was to be tolerated by the civil authority.

From the beginning of the colony, the individual churches had been established under the close supervision of the government. March 3, 1635, it was provided that all new churches, before being organized, should secure the approval of the magistrates and elders of the greater part of the churches in the colony. No member of any church organized without such authority could be admitted to the freedom of the commonwealth.[2] This provision, with the change that the church should have the approval of three or more magistrates, dwelling next, and of the elders of the neighboring churches, remained in force during the whole period.[3]

The churches were given a certain amount of independence, but even here they were closely guarded in their actions. By Liberty 95, the churches had authority "to exercise all the ordinances of God according to the scripture," to elect and depose their own officers, and to admit and dismiss members. Also no injunctions were to be placed on churches or members thereof except "the Institutions of the Lord." It was added in the later revisions that the officers chosen should be pious and orthodox.[4] Liberty 95 further provided that the churches could deal with their own members in a church

[1] *Platforms*, ch. xvii.

[2] *Mass. Col. Rec.*, vol. i. p. 168.

[3] *Laws*, 1660–72, p. 147; *Laws*, 1672–86, p. 43. While non-church-members might be admitted by law of 1664, no other church was recognized.

[4] *Laws*, 1660–72, p. 147; *Laws*, 1672–86, pp. 43–4, 46.

way. Magistrates, deputies and other officers were not exempt from this power, but Liberty 60 declared that no church censure should degrade or depose a man from any civil dignity, office, or authority he held in the commonwealth.[1] The excommunicated person, however, could be dealt with by civil authority.[2] No church member could plead his church relations as an exemption from the power of the state. Liberty 59 expressly declared that the commonwealth had power to deal with any church member in a way of civil justice, notwithstanding any church relation, office, or interest. But the civil authority was to go still farther and see that "the Peace, Ordinances and Rules of Christ" were "observed in every church according to his word."[3]

Not only did the civil power require that the church organization should be uniform, but it also required that the individual should give his support to that organization. Beginning with 1634 numerous laws were passed for the punishment of persons who absented themselves from church meetings.[4] Criticism of church teaching and opposition to church doctrine were also forbidden.[5] But religious obligation went further: the individual had to contribute to the maintenance of the church as well as to that of the government. With the very beginning of the colony the support of the ministers was provided for;[6] and this, with other church expenses, was the subject of

[1] *Laws*, 1660–72, p. 147; *Laws*, 1672–86, pp. 43–4; *Platforms*, ch. xiv; *Plain Dealing* (ed. by Trumbull, Boston, 1867), pp. 32–4.

[2] Ellis, *Puritan Age*, p. 210; *Mass. Col. Rec.*, vol. i, pp. 242, 271.

[3] Liberty, 58; *Laws*, 1660–72, p. 147; *Laws*, 1672–86, p. 44.

[4] *Mass. Col. Rec.*, vol. i, p. 140; vol. ii, p. 178; *Laws*, 1660–72, pp. 147–8; *Laws*, 1672–86, pp. 44–5.

[5] *Laws*, 1660–72, pp. 147–8; *Laws*, 1672–86, pp. 44–5.

[6] *Mass. Col. Rec.*, vol. i, p. 55.

many laws. If the individual did not willingly contribute according to his means, then he was to be assessed. The non-freemen and non-church-members were not exempt. The tax fell upon all alike.[1] A question involving these points came up before the General Court, October 14, 1657. The people of Ipswich had voted to give one hundred pounds towards either building or buying a house for Mr. Cobbett. The question was whether this vote bound all the inhabitants willing or unwilling, and the Court answered in the affirmative.[2]

With this conception of the relation between church and state, it is natural that the General Court should enact laws to maintain the church in all its purity and protect it against outside corruption and danger. This was not only the right of the Court but its express duty.[3] Such questions occupied a large portion of the time of both the legislature and the courts,[4] and some of the laws enacted will be treated later, although the religious controversies are beyond the scope of this work.

While the civil power supported and protected the church, it received in turn the co-operation and assistance of the ministers and elders. These two facts made the church a powerful influence in legislation and judicature. Among the ministers and elders were the best educated and the most capable men in the colony—such men as John Cotton, John Wilson, John Norton, Nathaniel Ward, and Increase Mather. In their election sermons the ministers often called the Court's

[1] *Mass. Col. Rec.*, vol. i, pp. 140-1; vol. ii, pp. 60, 209-10; *Laws*, 1660-72, pp. 147-8; *Laws*, 1672-86, pp. 44-5.

[2] *Mass. Col. Rec.*, vol. iv, pt. i, pp. 310-1. For account in full, see *Hutchinson Papers* (Publications of the Prince Society, Albany, 1865), vol. ii, pp. 1-25.

[3] *Platforms*, ch. xvii.

[4] Osgood, vol. i, pp. 215-7.

attention to needed legislation, and the Court in turn gave great weight to such advice.[1] The preparation of a code was entrusted, in 1639, to two ministers, John Cotton and Nathaniel Ward;[2] and the elders together with the magistrates were to review the code thus prepared before it was submitted to the freemen.[3] But the ministers and elders could act only as advisers in legislation. It had been agreed among the churches in 1632 that a person could not be a ruling elder and a magistrate at the same time.[4] But as advisers they had a great influence on legislation from the first. In 1633 they gave their opinion to the governor and magistrates on the statement of Roger Williams that the Patent was not valid;[5] and in 1634, in response to the General Court's request for their opinion, they said that the colony ought not to accept a general governor.[6] Such was the influence they had in the government during this whole period, except when the civil power was in the hands of Vane;[7] and the most striking examples of the weight and authority given to their opinions are to be found during the long struggle with the crown that finally resulted in the loss of the charter.[8]

The church then was the gateway to political privilege[9] until 1664 and even after that time a testimonial from the minister was required, which in all probability was not easily secured by those who stood outside

[1] Winthrop (ed. by Hosmer, New York, 1908), vol. i, pp. 134, 145; vol. ii, p. 37.

[2] *Ibid.* (Hosmer), vol. i, p. 323.

[3] *Ibid.* (Hosmer), vol. i, p. 324.

[4] *Ibid.* (Hosmer), vol. i, p. 83.

[5] *Ibid.* (Savage), vol. i, p. 145.

[6] *Ibid.* (Savage), vol. i, p. 183.

[7] Osgood, vol. i, p. 217.

[8] *Mass. Col. Rec.*, vol. iv, pt. ii, pp. 119, 316; vol. v, pp. 492-4.

[9] Suffrage in town meetings was not strictly limited to freemen except in the more important questions. Osgood, vol. i, p. 212.

the church. The civil power exercised supervision over and protected the church, and it received the church's moral support in return. The church's power, therefore, as a law-making factor, was due (1) to the conception of the relation between church and state and the responsibility of both to the will of God, and (2) to the personal influence of the ministers and elders.

LAWYERS

There was no class of trained attorneys who devoted their time to the practicc of law. It is true that some of the magistrates, as Winthrop, Bellingham, and Humphrey, had received a legal education in England, but these men were almost continuously in the magistracy, and there is no record of their having conducted cases.[1] Nathaniel Ward, for several years minister at Ipswich and author of the *Body of Liberties*, had been educated at Cambridge and had studied law.[2] According to his own statement, he had read almost all the common law of England and some statutes.[3] In the early years of the colony, parties to a controversy spoke for themselves, as a general rule;[4] but it was distinctly stated in Liberty 26 that every man who found himself unfit to plead his own cause in any court should have the liberty to employ any man to whom the court had no objection. But the advocate was to receive no fee, and the client was not exempted from answering in person such questions as the court might see fit to ask. The prohibition of fees

[1] Washburn, p. 50.

[2] Ward, *The Simple Cobler* (Boston, 1843), p. iii; Winthrop (Hosmer) vol. ii, pp. 48-9.

[3] *Simple Cobler*, p. 68.

[4] *Plain Dealing*, p. 86; Hutchinson, vol. i, p. 400.

seems to have been quietly dropped a few years later.[1] Although there were no trained attorneys to foment a controversy there were plenty of law suits, and a provision against barratry was enacted in the *Body of Liberties*.[2]

The lack of advocates led to the custom of going to the magistrates for *ex parte* statements and advice before the cause came up for trial. Nathaniel Ward, in preaching the election sermon at the General Court, held June 2, 1641, stated that the magistrates should not give private advice nor hear any man's cause before it came up in public. But when it was proposed, later in the session, to prohibit the magistrates from giving such advice, the order was opposed, and among the grounds of opposition it was urged that lawyers would have to be provided to direct men in their causes, accordingly no action was taken until several years later.[3] This seems to indicate that there was some opposition to professional attorneys, and the drift of events even before this time supports the same view.

Gradually, however, there arose a class of persons who devoted at least a portion of their time to the conducting of cases. These men doubtless paid some attention to the study of the law, but there was no fixed period of preparation required. Technical training was less necessary than later, because the forms of procedure were not intricate.[4] As time went on the advocate gained a place in the litigation of the colony. It became recognized that, if an evil, he was at least a necessary evil. His services seemed essential to the speedy and satisfactory ad-

[1] Whitmore, *Bibliog. Sketch*, p. 28.

[2] Liberty 34; *Laws*, 1660–72, p. 125; *Laws*, 1672–86, p. 9.

[3] Winthrop (Savage), vol. ii, pp. 42–3.

[4] Joseph Willard, *Address* (Lancaster, 1830), pp. 27–8.

ministration of justice. In 1649 it was provided that appeals should be made by the party or his attorney in writing. Also, after one month's publication, no one was to ask a magistrate's advice in regard to a case to be tried.[1] So common had it become to be represented by attorneys that, in 1663, it was deemed necessary to exclude all usual and common attorneys from seats as deputies in the General Court.[2] This prevented advocates from acting as judges upon cases they had tried in lower courts. Although the advocates were ignorant of technical law and had to be limited, in 1656, to one hour in pleading, so as not to take up the time of the court unduly,[3] yet it is reasonable to suppose that they knew far more law than their clients and that they greatly facilitated the administration of justice. This fact doubtless led to the further extension of their powers which is contained in an order of October 15, 1673.[4]

Regarding these earlier attorneys, who could hardly be termed lawyers, we have more or less information. In Middlesex, in 1652, Mr. Cogan appeared as attorney to Stephen Day, the first printer.[5] In 1654, in the case of Ridgway against Jordan, Amos Richardson appeared for the defendant; and in 1656 Edmund Goffe and Thomas Danforth appeared for the plaintiff in the case of John Glover against Henry Dunster, once president of Harvard College. But these men were not advocates alone; they were engaged in other kinds of business. John Cogan

[1] *Mass. Col. Rec.*, vol. ii, p. 279.

[2] *Ibid.*, vol. iv, pt. ii, p. 87; *Laws*, 1660–72, p. 224; *Laws*, 1672–86, p. 41.

[3] Washburn, p. 52.

[4] *Mass. Col. Rec.*, vol. iv, pt. ii, p. 563; *Laws*, 1672–86, p. 211.

[5] *The Memorial History of Boston* (ed. by Justin Winsor, Boston, 1880–81), vol. i, p. 455.

was a merchant and kept the first shop in Boston;[1] Amos Richardson was a tailor;[2] Goffe and Danforth had held office in the government, but neither of them were of the legal profession.[3] John Dunton, a bookseller and publisher, who visited the colony in 1686,[4] mentions two other attorneys, Mr. Watson and Dr. Bullivant. Mr. Watson was formerly a merchant in London, but was not successful; in Boston he passed as a solicitor. Here he became "as dextrous at splitting of causes as if he had been bred up an Attorneys Clerk." He became familiar with the "Quirks of the Law" and gained "the Reputation of a Wit."[5] Dr. Bullivant had lived in London, and in Boston he became well known both as a physician and an orator. He paid some attention to the laws of the colony, and a little later he was made Andros's attorney-general.[6]

But there had been two lawyers in the colony. One of these was Thomas Lechford, who had been educated in England and had become a member of Lincoln's Inn.[7] He came to the colony in 1637[8] and followed for a time the practice of the law. His methods were found unsatisfactory. At the quarter court held in Boston, September 3, 1639, it was ordered that "Mr. Thomas Lechford, for going to the jewry & pleading with them out of court" should be "debarred from pleading any man's cause" thereafter, except "his own." He was also "admonished not to presume to meddle beyond

[1] *Mem. Hist.*, vol. i, p. 540. [2] *Ibid.*, vol. ii, p. xxx.

[3] Willard, p. 28.

[4] Dunton, *Letters Written from New England* (Prince Society Pub., vol. iii, Boston, 1867), pp. x, xi.

[5] Dunton, pp. 89–90. [6] *Ibid.*, pp. 94–5.

[7] Palfrey, vol. i, p. 553.

[8] Washburn, pp. 53–4; *Plain Dealing*, p. 63.

what hee" should "bee called by the courte."[1] He seems to have disregarded this order, for we find that he was again before the quarter court, held at Boston, December 1, 1640. On this occasion he acknowledged that he had overshot himself, said he was sorry for it, and promised to attend to his own business and not meddle with controversies. He was consequently dismissed.[2] Soon after this he returned to England, where he published his work called *Plain Dealing*, in which he gives the colonists some advice in regard to their attitude toward professional attorneys: "But take heed, my breathern," says he, "despite not learning, nor the worthy Lawyers of either gown, lest you repent too late."[3]

The other lawyer was Thomas Morton, of Merry-Mount fame, who had been a kind of pettifogger of Furnival's Inn. Because of his practices at Mount Woolison, after he came to America, the Plymouth authorities had sent him back to England,[4] but he returned to Plymouth in 1630 and resumed his old festivities at Merry-Mount. The court of assistants, however, took the matter in hand at once, and September 7, 1630, they ordered him to be set in the bilboes and then sent to England.[5] He returned in 1644,[6] but was called before the court of assistants the same year on the charge of having misrepresented the colony in England.[7] After having been kept in prison several months[8] he was fined £100 and set at liberty. The purpose of his release was

[1] *Mass. Col. Rec.*, vol. i, p. 270. [2] *Ibid.*, vol. i, p. 310.

[3] *Plain Dealing*, p. 86. [4] Palfrey, vol. i, pp. 231-2.

[5] *Mass. Col. Rec.*, vol. i, pp. 74-5; Winthrop (Hosmer), vol. i, p. 53.

[6] Winthrop (Hosmer), vol. ii, p. 154.

[7] *Ibid.*, vol. ii, p. 194. [8] *Mass. Col. Rec.*, vol. ii, p. 90.

to give him an opportunity to leave the colony. He had been a charge to the country, but the assistants thought he ought not to be punished corporally, since he was old and crazy. Soon afterwards he went to "Acomenticus" and died there two years later, poor and despised.[1] Like Lechford, he left a book to posterity called *New English Canaan*.[2]

The lack of a professional class of lawyers evidently had a great deal to do with many of the innovations in the legal system during this period. The committee that drew up an answer to Dr. Child's petition in 1646 admitted their superficial knowledge of English law, saying: "If we had able lawyers amongst us, we might have been more exact."[3] It was not until several years after the loss of the first charter that the profession gained a suitable educational basis and an appropriate standing.

LAW BOOKS

There were few law books in the colony from which to draw information. In fact, this period witnessed the advent in England of the great writers who systematized and put into plain language the principles of the common law.[4] It took some time for these works to find their way into the colony, and it took longer still for them to have any pronounced effect upon the legal system. Yet it would seem that the colonists recognized quite early the value of such writings as guides, for we find the following order of November 11, 1647:

[1] Winthrop (Hosmer), vol. ii, p. 196.

[2] Prince Soc. Pub., vol. ix.

[3] *Hutchinson Papers*, vol. i, p. 227.

[4] Before this time the treatises were fragmentary and were written in Latin or in antiquated English. See Kent, *Commentaries on American Law*, lecture 22.

It is agreed by the Court, to the end that we may have better light for making and proceeding about laws, that there shall be these books following procured for the use of the Court from time to time: Two of Sir Edward Cooke upon Littleton; two of the Book of Entries; two of Sir Edward Cooke upon Magna Charta; two of the New Terms of the Law; two of Dalton's Justice of the Peace; two of Sir Edward Cook's Reports.[1]

The colonists, however, never considered the law of England binding, but felt themselves free to adopt just so much of it as suited their purpose. The general attitude in this matter appeared early in the history of the commonwealth, but it provoked a great deal of opposition from time to time on the part of some of the inhabitants. A party, led by Dr. Child, presented a petition to the General Court in 1646, praying that they might be governed by the laws of England and have the same civil, political, and religious privileges as were enjoyed in the mother country.[2] This petition aroused the indignation of the Court, and Child and his associates were called to answer for their presumption. Child argued that every corporation of England was subject to the laws of England. But it was answered that there was a difference between being subject "to the laws in general" as were the citizens in England and being subject "to some laws of state, proper to foreign plantations." It was pointed out that corporations, like the city of London, had "divers customs and by-laws differing from the common and statute laws of England." But the petitioners persisted in their contention and

[1] *Mass. Col. Rec.*, vol. ii, p. 212.

[2] Child, *New England's Jonas* (Boston, 1869), pp. 8-18; Winthrop Hosmer), vol. ii, p. 271.

were severely dealt with by the Court.[1] Many other controversies arose over the same question, but the authorities firmly maintained their position. In reference to the acts of Parliament for encouraging trade and navigation, the General Court said, October 2, 1678: "We humbly conceive, according to the usual sayings of the learned in the lawe, that the lawes of England are bounded within the fower seas, and doe not reach America."[2] But while English law was not regarded as binding, yet it was often referred to, and English writers were quoted for illustration or analogy in difficult questions.[3]

There were a number of publications of the laws of the colony. The first of these was the *Body of Liberties*, prepared mainly by Nathaniel Ward and printed in 1641 under the authority of the General Court.[4] For a long time the people had wished "a body of laws" and considered "their condition very unsafe, while so much power rested in the discretion of magistrates." But the project was opposed by "most of the magistrates and some of the elders" for two reasons: they thought that laws "which should arise *pro re nata* upon occasions" would be better for the colony; and they feared that they would have to "transgress the limits" of the charter by making laws repugnant to those of England. Laws which arose from practice and custom they did not consider "made" within the meaning of the prohibition. But finally the pressure became so great that the magis-

[1] Winthrop (Savage), vol. ii, pp. 340–59; *Mass. Col. Rec.*, vol. ii, pp. 196, 205, 241.

[2] *Mass. Col. Rec.*, vol. v, p. 200.

[3] Mass Hist. Colls., 4th ser., vol. vii, p. 132; *Hutch. Papers*, vol. ii, p. 5.

[4] Winthrop (Hosmer), vol. ii, pp. 48–9; *Mass. Col. Rec.*, vol. i, p. 346.

trates yielded, and the result was the code of 1641 mentioned above.[1] The first collection of the laws was issued in 1649, but unfortunately this edition has been lost, although we find many references to it.[2] There was also a revision of the laws published in 1660 and a further revision published in 1672.[3] In addition to these, the acts of the various sessions of the General Court were printed from time to time.[4]

While considering the law books in the colony, it must not be forgotten that the Scriptures were an infallible guide for both judge and legislator. At the General Court held May 25, 1636, a committee was appointed "to make a draught of lawes agreeable to the word of God." "In the meane tyme the magistrates & their associates" were to "determine all causes according to the laws" already "established & where there" was "noe law, then as neere the lawe of God as they" were able. "All business out of Court for which there" was "noe certaine rule" was to be "ordered & settled" by two or more members of the standing council "according to the rule of God's word."[5] The situation was clearly indicated in the *Body of Liberties*. Security in person, family and property was assured unless forfeited

> by virtue or equity of some express law of the Country warranting the same, established by a General Court and sufficiently published, or in case of the defect of a law in any particular case by the word of God. And in Capitall cases,

[1] Winthrop (Savage), vol. i, pp. 388–9.

[2] Whitmore, *Bibliog. Sketch*, p. 103.

[3] *Laws*, 1660–72, p. 1.

[4] *Ibid.*, pp. 219–60; *Laws*, 1672–86, pp. 199–355.

[5] *Mass. Col. Rec.*, vol. i, pp. 174–5.

or in cases concerning dismembering or banishment, according to that word to be judged by the Generall Court.[1]

It was also provided that "no custome or prescription" should prevail, in any moral cause, which could be proved "morrallie sinfull by the word of god."[2] These provisions remained in force during the Puritan ascendency[3] and explain the origin of many of the local laws.

English authorities were cited for illustration only, and English law was not regarded as binding except in so far as it was incorporated in the acts of the General Court. In the absence of such acts, not English judicial precedents, but the Scriptures were the subsidiary law.

[1] Liberty 1.

[2] Liberty 65.

[3] *Laws*, 1660–72, pp. 121, 186; *Laws*, 1672–86, pp. 1, 126.

CHAPTER II

The Law

CIVIL PROCEDURE

Little regard was paid to the forms of actions. The colonists had replevin, debt and trespass, and sometimes employed a special form of process to recover possession of real estate, but the most common form of action was that on the case.[1] At the first court of assistants, held at "Charlton," August 23, 1630, it was ordered that, "in all civil actions, the first process or summons by the beadle or his deputy" should "be directed by the Governor, or Deputy Governor, or some of the Assistants, being a justice of the peace; the next process" was "to be a capias or distringas att the discretion of the Court."[2] These terms, however, were loosely used; and it would seem that they came to mean summons and attachment, and that a court could grant such writs as the first process. The writ of replevin was also in use.[3] These writs were concise and were not issued in the king's name until 1662.[4]

At first litigation was very inexpensive, but so many actions were brought in the various courts that it became a great burden to the country. It was found

[1] Washburn, p. 48.

[2] *Mass. Col. Rec.*, vol. i, p. 74.

[3] *Laws*, 1660–72, p. 203; *Laws*, 1672–86, p, 162.

[4] *Mass. Col. Rec.*, vol. iv, pt. ii, p. 58; *Laws*, 1672–86, p. 161; Washburn, p. 48.

necessary, therefore, to advance the fees from time to time. September 25, 1634, the fee for entering an action was fixed at twelve pence,[1] but it was raised, November 20, 1637, to eighteen pence with an additional charge of two shillings for making every execution.[2] It was again advanced by order of September 27, 1642, which declared that every man had to pay ten shillings before his cause could be entered, unless the court should admit him *in forma pauperis*.[3] By order of November 11, 1647, in every action where the amount recovered was ten pounds or more there was to be an additional fee of five shillings, and when it was twenty pounds or more an additional fee of ten shillings. These additional fees were to be put in the judgment or execution, and the marshal was to account for the same to the treasurer.[4] No further change was made in this matter; but there were certain other minor payments connected with litigation, such as the fees paid to the clerk of writs.

The time for entry of actions was limited, in 1647, to the first day of the court,[5] and it was added, in 1665, that there should be double fees after the first forenoon of the session.[6] But summons and attachment, according to Liberty 21, had to be served six days before the session in order to be valid, unless the court had been called upon extraordinary occasion.[7] It was explained,

[1] *Mass. Col. Rec.*, vol. i, p. 129. [2] *Ibid.*, vol. i, p. 215.

[3] *Ibid.*, vol. ii, p. 28; *Laws*, 1660–72, p. 121; *Laws*, 1672–86, p. 2.

[4] *Mass. Col. Rec.*, vol. ii, p. 215; *Laws*, 1660–72, p. 121; *Laws*, 1672–86, p. 3.

[5] *Mass. Col. Rec.*, vol. ii, p. 219; *Laws*, 1660–72, p. 232; *Laws*, 1672–86, p. 2.

[6] *Mass. Col. Rec.*, vol. iv, pt. ii, p. 280; *Laws*, 1660–72, p. 232; *Laws*, 1672–86, p. 2.

[7] *Laws*, 1660–72, p. 124; *Laws*, 1672–86, p. 7.

however, in 1647, that the day upon which the summons or attachment was served and the day of appearance should both be counted.[1] But by order of 1685 all attachments in civil actions had to be served fourteen days before court.[2]

At first attachment and summons were granted at the discretion of the court; but it was provided, in 1644, that no attachment should be granted to a foreigner against an inhabitant unless he should give sufficient security to prosecute the case and insure such costs as the court might award.[3] Summons, however, proved unsuccessful in many cases, since various person chose to pay the small costs for non-appearance (thus gaining time to dispose of their property) rather than to risk a speedy trial. An order of 1650, therefore, gave the plaintiff his choice between summons and attachment.[4] It had already been provided, in 1644, that in all attachments of goods, chattels, lands or hereditaments legal notice should be given to the party or left in writing at his house or abode.[5] And until 1675 attachments of either person and property were returnable to the courts; but an order of that year made it legal for the marshal or constable to make his return upon the back of the writ and deliver the same sealed to the plaintiff, when demanded, and a copy to the defendant, if he desired it.[6]

[1] *Mass. Col. Rec.*, vol. ii, p. 194.

[2] *Ibid.*, vol. v, p. 503; *Laws*, 1672–86, p. 330.

[3] *Mass. Col. Rec.*, vol. ii, p. 80; *Laws*, 1660–72, p. 124; *Laws*, 1672–86, p. 7.

[4] *Mass. Col. Rec.*, vol. iv, p. i, p. 5; *Laws*, 1660–72, p. 124; *Laws*, 1672–86, p. 7.

[5] *Mass. Col. Rec.*, vol. ii, p. 80; *Laws*, 1660–72, p. 124; *Laws*, 1672–86, p. 7.

[6] *Mass. Col. Rec.*, vol. v, p. 29.

For several years there were no written declarations. The pleadings were long and confused, and defendants often complained that they did not know what to answer or what witnesses to summon before they appeared in court. But an order of 1647 required the plaintiff or his attorney to draw up a declaration and deliver the same to the recorder or clerk at least three days before the session, so that the defendant would have time to put in his answer in writing and summon his witnesses according to the nature of the declaration.[1] A further provision to remove confusion was made in 1651, requiring the summons or attachment to express whether the plaintiff sued in his own name, or as executor, administrator, assignee, attorney, guardian or agent. If the plaintiff failed to do this and exception was taken before the issue was joined, he was liable for the costs.[2] An assignee had the same rights as the original creditor, if the assignment was made upon the back of the instrument.[3] Persons under twenty-one had to be represented by their parents, masters or guardians,[4] and married women could not sue or be sued without their husbands.[5]

Penalties for non-appearance were defined in the order of May 22, 1650. The plaintiff, if he failed to appear, was to be "non-suited," and in all cases the party present was to have costs against the party absent; but the parties were to be permitted to try the case at the

[1] *Mass. Col. Rec.*, vol. ii, p. 219.

[2] *Ibid.*, vol. iv, pt. i, pp. 38–9; *Laws*, 1660–72, p. 124; *Laws*, 1672–86, p. 8.

[3] *Laws*, 1660–72, p. 125; *Laws*, 1672–86, p. 10.

[4] *Mass. Col. Rec.*, vol. iv, pt. ii, p. 397; *Laws*, 1672–86, p. 2.

[5] *Hutch. Papers*, vol. i, p. 235.

same court, if they so agreed. For his new entry, in such case, the plaintiff had to pay half-fees.[1]

At first both parties were given a great deal of scope in making claims and pleas.[2] Technical points and pleas in abatement were not usual. Lechford complained that most matters were tried and ended the same court.[3] And a provision in the laws of 1660 and 1672 declared that "no summons, pleading, judgment, or any kind of proceeding in the courts or course of justice, shall be abated, arrested or reversed, upon any kind of circumstantial errours or mistakes, if the person and cause be rightly understood, & intended by the Court."[4] But, according to an order of 1649, if either party had asked advice of a magistrate or judge before whom the case afterwards came up, it could be pleaded by way of bar. The plaintiff, if guilty, could not prosecute his case at the next court and had to pay full costs to the defendant. The defendant was to forfeit ten shillings for each like offense.[5]

There were few rules of evidence. Any magistrate or commissioner authorized by the General Court was given power in 1647 to take the testimony of persons over fourteen years of age. But if the witness resided within ten miles of the court, he was to be present for further examination. Witnesses, however, could demand their fees before attending.[6] Another order, passed in

[1] *Mass. Col. Rec.*, vol. iv, pt. i, p. 4; *Laws*, 1660–72, p. 168; *Laws*, 1672–86, p. 87.

[2] Liberty 55 (dropped later, *Cf. Bibliog. Sketch*, p. 28).

[3] *Plain Dealing*, p. 86.

[4] *Laws*, 1660–72, p. 124; *Laws*, 1672–86, p. 7.

[5] *Mass. Col. Rec.*, vol. ii, pp. 279–80; *Laws*, 1660–72, p. 141; *Laws*, 1672–86, p. 34.

[6] *Mass. Col. Rec.*, vol. ii, pp. 204–5; *Laws*, 1660–72, pp. 101–2; *Laws*, 1672–86, p. 158.

1650, provided that all testimony should be presented in writing, but it had to be attested before a magistrate or, if the witness resided within ten miles, attested in court upon oath. The reason given for this provision was that the clerks had found it difficult to make a perfect copy of oral testimony.[1] These provisions made it possible to examine precedents and to determine their applicability, since an earlier law, passed in 1639, had provided that every judgment, with all the evidence, should be recorded in a book, to be kept to posterity.[2]

As to the weight of evidence, the court and jury, according to an order of 1657, were to see that the plaintiff proved his case; otherwise the judgment was to be for the defendant.[3] Account books were admitted as evidences of debt. An order of 1669 limited the validity of book debts to three years;[4] but the time was extended by various orders, and in 1679, this limitation was wholly repealed.[5] The court of assistants decided in 1684 that a dead man's books, though well kept, were not legal evidence.[6] In civil cases wives could not testify for or against their husbands.[7] With these restrictions, the whole plea and evidence was to be presented before the case was committed to the jury, for, according to an order of 1665, no after plea or evidence would be admitted.[8]

[1] *Mass. Col. Rec.*, vol. iv, pt. i, p. 27.

[2] *Ibid.*, vol. i, p. 275; Liberty 64; *Laws*, 1660–72, p. 188; *Laws*, 1672–86, p. 129.

[3] *Mass. Col. Rec.*, vol. iv, pt. i, pp. 290–1.

[4] *Ibid.*, vol. iv, pt. ii, p. 422; *Laws*, 1660–72, p. 261 g; *Laws*, 1672–86, p. 37.

[5] *Laws*, 1672–86, p. 266.

[6] Martin against Lake, *Records of the Court of Assistants* (ed. by Noble, 2 vols., Boston, 1901–4), vol. i, p. 269.

[7] *Mass. Col. Rec.*, vol. iv, pt. ii, p. 306.

[8] *Laws*, 1660–72, p. 232; *Laws*, 1672–86, p. 2.

The first juries mentioned were those called by the coroner;[1] but it is certain that juries were in use in the early days of the colony in civil as well as in criminal cases. Lechford says that "matters of debt, trespass, and upon the case and equity, yea and of heresie also are tried by a jury."[2] Liberty 29 provided that in all actions at law the plaintiff and defendant, by mutual consent, could decide whether they would have their case referred to the bench or to a jury, except where the law provided otherwise.[3] The advisability of juries was questioned, however, for on September 27, 1642, a committee was appointed to consider whether it would be better to retain or dismiss juries in the trial of causes.[4] And on May 26, 1652, a law was passed providing that all civil actions should be tried without a jury, unless either the plaintiff or defendant should desire one. The party that made the request had to pay the extra fee of twenty shillings for each action, and this amount was to be assessed in costs upon the party against whom judgment was rendered. In such cases the jurors might be taken out of the three or four next towns, and the party making the request had to give notice to the secretary or clerk of the court four days before the session. A party might also have a jury in special courts by conforming to certain rules.[5] The General Court at its next session, October 19, 1652, passed an order in the following words: "The law about juries is repealed, and juries are in force againe."[6] What law this order referred to is not clear, but since it was passed at the second session

[1] *Records of Court of Assistants*, vol. ii, pp. 6-7.

[2] *Plain Dealing*, p. 85.

[3] *Laws*, 1660-72, p. 197; *Laws*, 1672-86, p. 152.

[4] *Mass. Col. Rec.*, vol. ii, p. 28.

[5] *Ibid.*, vol. iv, pt. i, p. 81. [6] *Ibid.*, vol. iv, pt. i, p. 107.

of 1652, it would seem that it was meant to repeal the intricate order of May 26, 1652, passed at the first session. This is rendered the more probable by the fact that neither of these orders is contained in the revisions of 1660 and 1672. There is no record of the suspension of juries in either civil or criminal cases, nor did the law of May 26, 1652, on its face, do away with jury trial in civil cases. It required, however, a trial without a jury in the absence of a request from either of the parties, and it is likely that it was this requirement, together with the additional fees and inconveniences, which the order of October 19 was intended to sweep away.

In view of the fact that some of the towns had complained of the unequal burden, an order of October 17, 1649, provided that the clerk or secretary of each court should apportion jurymen among the various towns according to population.[1] According to the revisions of 1660 and 1672 all juries serving at the court of assistants in Boston were to be summoned out of the counties of Suffolk and Middlesex respectively.[2] In summoning jurors, the secretary or clerk of each court sent warrants to the constables of the several towns under the jurisdiction of that court. The constables gave notice to the freemen,[3] who elected the number of jurors apportioned to the town where they dwelt.[4] No juror could be compelled to serve in civil cases more than one ordinary court in a year,[5] and no person under twenty-one was eligible.[6]

[1] *Mass. Col. Rec.*, vol. ii, p. 285; *Laws*, 1660-72, p. 167; *Laws*, 1672-86, p. 86.

[2] *Laws*, 1660-72, p. 167; *Laws*, 1672-86, p. 86.

[3] *Laws*, 1660-72, p. 167; *Laws*, 1672-86, p. 86.

[4] Liberty 50; *Laws*, 1660-72, p. 167; *Laws*, 1672-86, p. 86.

[5] Liberty 49; *Laws*, 1660-72, p. 168; *Laws*, 1672-86, p. 87.

[6] Liberty 53; *Laws*, 1660-72, p. 121; *Laws*, 1672-86, p. 1.

Parties could challenge jurymen; but there were certain limitations upon this privilege, as is indicated in the case of the wife of Francis Weston before the church of Salem in 1637.[1] Lechford states that, although challenge could be made before a juror was sworn, yet it was hindered by the fact that there was but one jury in a court for the trial of causes and all parties were not present at the swearing.[2] Liberty 30 declared that either plaintiff or defendant could challenge members of the jury, and if such challenge were found just and reasonable by the bench or the rest of the jury, others had to be summoned to fill the vacancies. This made the bench or the rest of the jury judges of the grounds upon which jurors could be challenged; and thus it remained.[3]

As to the verdict, Lechford says that, although "the magistrates may judge what is law, and what is equall, and some of the Chief Ministers informe what is heresie, yet the Jury may find a general verdict, if they please; and seldome is there any speciall verdict found by them, with deliberate arguments made thereupon."[4] By Liberty 31, where the evidence was so obscure or defective that the jury could not give a positive verdict, it could bring in a *non liquet* or a special verdict. An order of June 14, 1642, provided that the jury should find the matter of fact with damages and costs, according to the evidence, and the judges should give the sentence of law upon it, or that the judges might direct the jury to find according to the law. But if there should be "matter of

[1] *Coll. Essex Institute*, vol. i, pp. 40–41.

[2] *Plain Dealing*, p. 85.

[3] *Laws*, 1660–72, p. 197; *Laws*, 1672–86, p. 152.

[4] *Plain Dealing*, p. 85.

apparent equity, as the forfeiture of an obligation, breach of covenant without damage, or the like, the bench" should "determine such matters of equity."[1] A law of May 6, 1657, declared that it was the duty of the jury, if they understood the law in the case, to find accordingly, but if some of them did not, the whole jury could present a special verdict. *Non liquet* verdicts, however, were not to be found thereafter.[2] The General Court was asked, October 15, 1679, if, when a case had been committed to the jury, they ought not to bring in their verdict upon the merits of the case, without evading the issue upon any circumstance in way of bar or non-suit, unless such had been allowed by the bench at the time, and the court answered in the affirmative.[3] But by Liberty 76 the jury was permitted to take counsel of any one in open court before rendering their verdict.[4]

It had been provided that when the bench and jury disagreed in any verdict the case could be removed to the General Court.[5] Later, such cases were to be removed from the county court to the court of assistants.[6] But the statute of May 15, 1672, took away the power of the bench to refuse the verdict of the jury in civil cases, and declared that, in all county courts, after the bench had instructed the jury, the verdict finally given should be accepted and judgment entered accordingly. The procedure was to be the same in the court of assist-

[1] *Mass. Col. Rec.*, vol. ii, p. 21; *Laws*, 1660–72, p. 167; *Laws*, 1672–86, p. 86.

[2] *Mass. Col. Rec.*, vol. iv, pt. i, p. 291; *Laws*, 1660–72, p. 167; *Laws*, 1672–86, p. 87.

[3] *Mass. Col. Rec.*, vol. iv, pt. ii, pp. 243–4; *Laws*, 1672–86, p. 272.

[4] *Laws*, 1660–72, p. 168; *Laws*, 1672–86, p. 87.

[5] Liberty 31.

[6] *Laws*, 1660–72, p. 167; *Laws*, 1672–86, p. 87.

ants, unless upon apparent corruption or error "the party cast" should in open court attaint the jury[1] and give bond and security to prosecute them at the next session. In that case a jury of twenty-four men was to be summoned by the clerk of the court to pass upon the attaint. If there was found to be manifest error or mistake, the party complaining was to recover his full damage from the other party to the original suit. If the attainted jury were acquitted, they were to have double costs from the accusing party, and their verdict and the judgment of the former court were to be valid and execution was to be issued accordingly. In case of bribery, conspiracy or other corruption found against the attainted jury, they were to be punished by fine or imprisonment, according to the degree of the offense.[2] The abuse of the privilege of attaint[3] gave occasion for the order of September 10, 1684, which provided that in all attaints the party should set forth in writing the cause and argument sustaining it. If the verdict of the former jury was confirmed, he was to pay a fine of ten pounds to the country and forty shillings apiece to the attainted jury, and the other party was to have double costs and also double interest, because of delay in receiving his just debt according to the former verdict. In case the jury had been charged with corruption and acquitted, they could, jointly or severally, prosecute the action of slander; and the party bringing the attaint was to be liable to the country for such further fine as the court should judge meet.[4]

[1] Attaint had ceased in England. Blackstone, *Commentaries*, vol. iii, p. 404.

[2] *Mass. Col., Rec.*, vol. iv, pt. ii, pp. 508-9; *Laws*, 1672-86, pp. 201-2.

[3] Cases of attaint in *Records of Court of Assistants*, vol. i.

[4] *Mass. Col. Rec.*, vol. v, pp. 449-50; *Laws*, 1672-86, pp. 319-20.

By a provision in the *Body of Liberties* which remained permanent, the plaintiff was permitted to withdraw his action or be "non-suited" in all causes, brought to any court, providing he made use of the privilege before the jury had returned a verdict. In this event, he had to pay full costs and charges to the defendant, but could renew his suit at another court.[1]

According to an act of November 12, 1644, a judgment against a defendant absent was not to be executed before the plaintiff had given security for loss or costs, if the judgment should be reversed within a year or such further time as the court might permit.[2] And an order of October 18, 1654, made invalid the sale, alienation, or assignment of any judgment or execution;[3] but the General Court resolved, in answer to a question submitted October 12, 1681, that, in case of the death of a party against whom judgment was granted, but before execution had been taken out, the judgment should stand in force against his heirs, executors or administrators. The court added, however, that the person against whom the execution came should be at liberty to have the same reviewed.[4]

If the party against whom judgment had been rendered had any new evidence or other new matter to plead, he could request a new trial in the same court upon a bill of review.[5] Provision for appeal had been made as early as 1635,[6] and Liberty 36 declared that the "party cast"

[1] Liberty 28; *Laws*, 1660–72, p. 122; *Laws*, 1672–86, p. 3.

[2] *Mass. Col. Rec.*, vol. ii, p. 80; *Laws*, 1672–86, p. 7.

[3] *Mass. Col. Rec.*, vol. iv, pt. i, p. 202; *Laws*, 1660–72, p. 47; *Laws*, 1672–86, p. 85.

[4] *Mass. Col. Rec.*, vol. v, p. 323; *Laws*, 1672–86, p. 188.

[5] *Laws*, 1660–72, p. 197; *Laws*, 1672–86, p. 152.

[6] *Mass. Col. Rec.*, vol. i, p. 169.

in an inferior court could appeal to the court of assistants, provided he tendered his appeal and put in security to prosecute it before the court was ended and within six days gave bond for what his adversary might recover against him. The liberty of appeal was greatly abused; accordingly an order of November 11, 1647, required the appellant to record, on the day of the judgment, the appeal together with a brief statement of the reasons therefor, and to give, during that court, security sufficient to cover all costs and future judgments.[1] But the practice of taking out appeals in order to gain time became so common that it was ordered, May 7, 1651, that any one failing to prosecute an appeal should forfeit, besides his bond to the other party, forty shillings to the country.[2] The appellant had already been required by statute of May 2, 1649, to "give to some one of the judges from whome he did appeal the grounds and reason of his appeal six days before the beginning of that court to which he did appeale";[3] but by order of October 14, 1685, this time was extended to fourteen days.[4]

Upon petition the General Court could take cognizance of any case either in first instance or after trial in a lower court; but it usually exercised such power only (1) when the circumstances were peculiar and the law did not furnish an adequate remedy, or (2) where its judgment would be in the nature of a commutation or pardon.

In addition to those already mentioned, there was

[1] *Mass. Col. Rec.*, vol. ii, p. 219; *Laws*, 1660–72, p. 122; *Laws*, 1672–86, p. 4.

[2] *Mass. Col. Rec.*, vol. iv, pt. i, p. 38; *Laws*, 1660–72, p. 122; *Laws*, 1672–86. p. 4.

[3] *Mass. Col. Rec.*, vol. ii, p. 279; *Laws*, 1660–72, p. 122; *Laws*, 1672–86. p. 4.

[4] *Mass. Col. Rec.*, vol. v, p. 503; *Laws*, 1672–86, p. 330.

still another method of reviewing cases in higher courts. In 1676 the court of assistants decided that the liberty of appeal extended to the plaintiff when he was successful in the lower court but was not satisfied with the judgment. In this particular case the court affirmed the former judgment and added to it "tenn pounds more with Costs of Court."[1]

Costs did not follow the judgment as a matter of course but, according to the statute of May 20, 1642, were to be assessed against either party at the discretion of the court.[2] In case of voluntary trespass, however, where the offender had either paid or offered to pay the damage, the plaintiff, according to the order of May 22, 1650, could recover no costs incurred in the suit.[3]

Execution was taken out after final judgment. By order of November 11, 1647, certain kinds of property were exempt. The marshal was not to levy on any man's necessary bedding, apparel, tools, arms, or indispensable household implements, but in such cases was to "levy [on] his land or person according to law."[4] If any one should die after he had obtained judgment but before he had taken out execution or the execution had been satisfied, his executor or administrator, according to the act of October 18, 1654, could take out or renew the execution.[5] To prevent unnecessary delay, it was ordered, March 11, 1659, that, unless the defendant was

[1] Greely against Young, *Records of Court of Assistants*, vol. i, p. 81.

[2] *Mass. Col. Rec.*, vol. ii, p. 3.

[3] *Ibid.*, vol. iv, pt. ii, pp. 4-5; *Laws*, 1660-72, p. 131; *Laws*, 1672-86, p. 18.

[4] *Mass. Col. Rec.*, vol. ii, p. 204; *Laws*, 1660-72; p. 174; *Laws*, 1672-86, p. 104.

[5] *Mass. Col. Rec.*, vol. iv, pt. i, p. 202; *Laws*, 1660-72, p. 167; *Laws*, 1672-86, pp. 85-6.

a stranger, all executions not taken out and executed within one month after judgment should be void, unless the court should extend the time in any particular case.[1] In order to put a stop to the practice of getting rid of property before execution had been granted, a statute of October 15, 1650, provided that goods attached should not be released upon appearance or judgment, but only after the execution had been discharged; also that any surety for appearance should not be released from his bond until the execution was satisfied or the person surrendered into the hands of the marshal.[2] But the law provided no adequate method of compelling a bondsman to pay when he failed to appear and secure release. It was, therefore, ordered, May 15, 1672, that in such cases his bond should be declared forfeited upon non-appearance, and judgment granted against both the defendant and his surety and execution issued accordingly, which should remain in force one month after judgment.[3]

Liberty 33 declared that no man should be arrested or imprisoned upon execution or judgment for any debt or fine, if his estate would give satisfaction;[4] but if not, he could be arrested and imprisoned, to be kept at his own, not the plaintiff's expense, until satisfaction should be made, unless the court should otherwise provide. By order of May 7, 1662, where the debtor should take an oath before a magistrate that he was not worth five pounds and the plaintiff would not pay for his mainte-

[1] *Mass. Col. Rec.*, vol. iv, pt. i, pp. 365–6; *Laws*, 1660–72, p. 194; *Laws*, 1672–86, p. 144.

[2] *Mass. Col. Rec.*, vol. iv, pt. i, p. 27; *Laws*, 1660–72, p. 194; *Laws*, 1672–86, p. 144.

[3] *Mass. Col. Rec.*, vol. iv, pt. ii, p. 509; *Laws*, 1672–86, p. 202.

[4] "Except in special contracts, or in the Law of Paiments." *Laws*, 1660–72, p. 123, and *Laws*, 1672–86, p. 6.

nance, he could be discharged by the keeper.[1] In case of imprisonment for debt, a statute of October 18, 1654, gave the keeper of the prison the same power of taking bail after commitment as the marshal had before commitment.[2]

CRIMINAL PROCEDURE

Many of the provisions noted above applied to criminal as well as to civil procedure, and a mere reference to them as occasion requires will be sufficient. The age at which a person was amenable to criminal process varied. The order of October 14, 1668, which provided that parties in civil actions should be at least twenty-one years old, declared that in all criminal cases every person, whether younger or older, should be required to answer in his own person for his misdemeanors, and could "also informe & present any misdemeanour to any magistrate, grand juryman, or court."[3] According to the revisions of 1660 and 1672, the age of discretion, which would mean the age of liability for crime, was fourteen,[4] but there were a number of exceptions to this rule. For heresy[5] and arson,[6] it was sixteen, and for capital crimes it varied from fourteen to sixteen.[7]

There were two ways of bringing an accused person before the court: (1) by arrest and (2) by summons after indictment by a grand jury. As a general rule, a

[1] *Mass. Col. Rec.*, vol. iv, pi. ii, p. 42; *Laws*, 1672-86, pp. 6, 128.

[2] *Mass. Col. Rec.*, vol. iv, pt. i, p. 208; *Laws*, 1660-72, p. 227; *Laws*, 1672-86, p. 7.

[3] *Mass. Col. Rec.*, vol. iv, pt. ii, p. 397.

[4] *Laws*, 1660-72, p. 171; *Laws*, 1672-86, p. 91.

[5] *Laws*, 1660-72, p. 154; *Laws*, 1672-86, p. 59.

[6] *Laws*, 1660-72, p. 152; *Laws*, 1672-86, p. 52.

[7] *Laws*, 1660-72, pp. 128-9; *Laws*, 1672-86, pp. 14-16.

person could not be arrested without warrant. It was declared, May 19, 1658, that no constable could "apprehend any person by order of any magistrate without warrant in writing." But there were a number of exceptions. The constable was authorized "to speede away all hues and crys, to effect & to signe them, where no magistrate is neere at hand, against theeves, robbers, murders, manslayers, peace breakers, & other capitall offenders, on penalty of forty shillings for neglect in capitall crimes." He could "apprehend without warrant" for drunkenness, swearing, Sabbath-breaking, lying, vagrancy, and night-walking, when he caught persons in the act or received immediate information of their committing such offences. These persons he was to keep in custody until he could bring them before a magistrate.[1] By a provision of the revisions of 1660 and 1672, where no magistrate was at hand, Quakers could be "apprehended without warrant" by any constable, commissioner or selectman, and conveyed from constable to constable until brought before the nearest magistrate.[2]

After arrest, either with or without warrant, the accused was brought before a magistrate. Liberty 18 declared that no man should be imprisoned before sentence, if he could tender sufficient bail to insure his appearance and good behavior, except in capital crimes, contempts in open court, or in those cases where the court should deny bail.[3] Later revisions added to this list of exceptions arson, heresy, and Quakerism.[4] Bond

[1] *Mass. Col. Rec.*, vol. iv, pt. i, pp. 324-5; *Laws*, 1660-72, p. 139; *Laws*, 1672-86, p. 31.

[2] *Laws*, 1660-72, p. 156; *Laws*, 1672-86, p. 61.

[3] *Laws*, 1660-72, p. 160; *Laws*, 1672-86, p. 74.

[4] *Laws*, 1660-72, pp. 152, 154, 156; *Laws*, 1672-86, pp. 52, 59, 61.

for appearance was made out to the marshal or the constable.[1] Every person charged with crime, "whether in prison or under Bail" was to be heard at the next court that had jurisdiction, if it could "be done without prejudice of Justice".[2] It was the duty of the prison-keepers to present from time to time a list of the prisoners to such courts as had cognizance of their crimes.[3]

Grand juries were probably in use very nearly from the beginning. According to Winthrop, as early as 1633 a "great jury" "found ignoramus" upon the indictment of Capt. John Stone for adultery.[4] By order of March 4, 1634, there were to be two grand juries summoned every year, one in March and the other in September, to inform the court of breaches of any order or other misdemeanor of which they should know or hear.[5] The first grand jury summoned under this order was in attendance at the General Court September 1, 1635. It presented more than "one hundred offences and, among others, some of the magistrates."[6] "Twice a yeare," says Lechford, "in the said great quarter Courts held before the generall Courts, are two grand juries sworne for the Jurisdiction, one for one Court, and the other for the other."[7] But by order of June 2, 1641, grand jurymen summoned for September were to serve also the following March and were to receive their charge in September.[8] Liberty 49 declared that grand jurymen should

[1] *Laws*, 1660–72, p. 203; *Laws*, 1672–86, p. 162.

[2] *Laws*, 1660–72, p. 144; *Laws*, 1672–86, p. 38.

[3] *Laws*, 1672–86, p. 128.

[4] Winthrop (Savage), vol. i, pp. 132–3.

[5] *Mass. Col. Rec.*, vol. i, p. 143.

[6] Winthrop (Savage), vol. i, p. 198.

[7] *Plain Dealing*, p. 84.

[8] *Mass. Col. Rec.*, vol. i, p. 329.

serve at least two courts together; and such was the permanent arrangement.[1]

Grand juries were summoned to the various courts in the same manner as petty juries,[2] and, according to Lechford, they were "charged to enquire and present offences reduced, by the Governour, who" gave "the charge most an-end under the Heads of the ten Commandments."[3] Of course, it was impossible for the governor to give the charge to all the grand juries after the courts became numerous. A provision of the laws of 1660 and 1672, which incorporated a portion of the order of 1634, already referred to, required grand juries to present all "misdemeanours" which they knew or heard were committed within the court's jurisdiction,[4] and an oath to this effect was prescribed.[5] But by Liberty 61 no juror or any person whatsoever was "bound to inform present or reveale any private crime or offence, wherein there" was "no perill or danger to" the colony.[6] Just as a petty jury, a grand jury was permitted to return a special verdict.[7]

A grand jury could indict persons before as well as after arrest. It was ordered, November 4, 1646, that any person, not in durance and indicted of a capital crime, who refused to surrender his person to some magistrate within one month after the last of three proclamations, publicly made in the town where he usually dwelt, one month intervening between proclamation and proclama-

[1] *Laws*, 1660–72, p. 168; *Laws*, 1672–86, p. 87.

[2] *Laws*, 1660–72, p. 167; *Laws*, 1672-86, p. 86.

[3] *Plain Dealing*, p. 84.

[4] *Laws*, 1660–72, p. 167; *Laws*, 1672–86, p. 86.

[5] *Laws*, 1660–72, p. 206; *Laws*, 1672–86, p. 167.

[6] *Laws*, 1660–72, p. 167; *Laws*, 1672-86, p. 86.

[7] *Laws*, 1660–72, p. 167; *Laws*, 1672–86, p. 72.

tion, should forfeit his lands and goods to the use of the common treasury, till he made his "lawfull appearance."[1] And a statute of May 22, 1650, declared that, if any person, presented by a grand jury or summoned by a magistrate to answer for any crime, did not make his appearance upon the third call, as aforesaid, he should be proceeded against for contempt, unless he had been prevented by the hand of God.[2] After 1662 indictments were in the king's name.[3]

The rights of the individual were insured to a certain extent by an act of May 26, 1652, which declared that no person should "be indicted, presented, informed against, or complained of, to any Courte or magistrate," except within a year after the offense. But this limitation was not to extend to capital offenses, to those involving the loss of limb or banishment, to treason or conspiracy against the commonwealth, or to "fellonies above tenn shillings." Nor was it to extend to wrongs against a man's person or his wife, children, servants, or estate, real or personal.[4]

According to Liberty 29, the accused, when brought to trial, could request a jury, unless the law had provided otherwise.[5] Most of the provisions noted above in regard to juries in civil cases apply here. Jurors could be challenged;[6] the jury was to decide matters of fact, and

[1] *Mass. Col. Rec.*, vol. ii, p. 182; *Laws*, 1660–72, p. 129; *Laws*, 1672–86, p. 16.

[2] *Mass. Col. Rec.*, vol. iv, pt. i, p. 4; *Laws*, 1660–72, p. 168; *Laws*, 1672–86, p. 88.

[3] *Mass. Col. Rec.*, vol. iv, pt. ii, p. 58.

[4] *Mass. Col. Rec.*, vol. iv, pt. i, pp. 81–82; *Laws*, 1660–72, p. 163; *Laws*, 1672–86, p. 79.

[5] *Laws*, 1660–72, p. 197; *Laws*, 1672–86, p. 152.

[6] Liberty 30; *Laws*, 1660–72, p. 197; *Laws*, 1672–86, p. 152.

the bench questions of law;[1] jurors could take advice in open court;[2] they had to be twenty-one years of age;[3] and juries summoned to the court of assistants were to be taken out of the counties of Suffolk and Middlesex respectively.[4] But a number of the provisions require special consideration. According to a statute of May 14, 1634, no person could be tried for a crime involving the penalty of death or banishment, except by a jury summoned for that purpose or by the General Court.[5] This provision is contained in the laws of 1660 and 1672, as follows: "No tryal shall pass upon any man for life or banishment in any inferior court, but by a special jury summoned for that purpose."[6] The right of the accused to demand a jury in such instances is probably all that is intended here, since persons were permitted after this time to refer the question of their guilt to the bench.[7] The usual procedure was to bring the prisoner to the bar where he was to plead guilty or not guilty to the indictment. If guilty, the matter rested in the hands of the bench; but if not guilty, the accused was permitted either to "put himself for tryall on God & the Country" or to refer "himself for his tryal to the Bench."[8] When summoned in life and banishment cases, the exemption that

[1] *Mass. Col. Rec.*, vol. iv, pt. i, p. 191; *Laws*, 1660-72, p. 167; *Laws*, 1672-86, p. 86.

[2] Liberty 76; *Laws*, 1660-72, p. 168; *Laws*, 1672-86, p. 87.

[3] Liberty 53; *Laws*, 1660-72, p. 121; *Laws*, 1672-86, p. 1.

[4] *Laws*, 1660-72, p. 167; *Laws*, 1672-86, 9. 86.

[5] *Mass. Col. Rec.*, vol. i, p. 118.

[6] *Laws*, 1660-72, p. 167; *Laws*, 1672-86, p. 86.

[7] Case of Walter Gendall, *Records of Court of Assistants* (referred to hereafter as "*Rec. Assist.*"), vol. i, p. 102. Other cases in the same volume.

[8] Cases in *Rec. Assist.*, vol. i.

jurors could not be required to attend more than one ordinary court a year did not apply.[1]

In regard to evidence, the order of November 11, 1647, which provided a method of taking the testimony of any person fourteen years of age outside of court, also declared that the same method could be used in criminal cases. But in capital crimes all witnesses had to be present, even though they resided over ten miles from the court.[2] Liberty 47 declared that no man should be put to death without the testimony of two or three witnesses, or the equivalent.[3] What "the equivalent" came to mean is worthy of note. By order of November 4, 1646, one witness was sufficient to convict a person of a capital crime, in case he had refused to surrender to a magistrate, without good cause.[4] In a case before the court of assistants, in 1673, confession before trial "together with one evidence" was sufficient, although the accused denied the charge on trial.[5] And in 1681 in the same court confession alone was sufficient.[6] Torture was forbidden by Liberty 45 as a means of forcing a man to confess a crime against himself or against another, except when it was very apparent after conviction in a capital case that there were confederates. Even then the torture was not to be barbarous or inhuman.[7] As in civil cases the burden of proof rested upon the plaintiff,

[1] *Laws*, 1660-72, p. 168; *Laws*, 1672-86, p. 87.

[2] *Mass. Col. Rec.*, vol. ii, pp. 204-5; *Laws*, 1660-72, pp. 201-2; *Laws*, 1672-86, p. 158.

[3] *Laws*, 1660-72, p. 201; *Laws*, 1672-86, p. 157.

[4] *Mass. Col. Rec.*, vol. ii, p. 182; *Laws*, 1660-72, p. 129; *Laws*, 1672-86, p. 16.

[5] Case of Benj. Goads, *Rec. Assist.*, vol. i, p. 10.

[6] Case of Maria, Negress, *ibid.*, vol. i, p. 198.

[7] *Laws*, 1660-72, p. 187; *Laws*, 1672-86, p. 129.

so in criminal cases the accused, according to act of May 6, 1657, was presumed to be innocent until proven guilty.[1] Also the provision in regard to technicalities applied in criminal as well as in civil procedure.[2] But the rules differed when it came to witness fees. In criminal cases these were to be paid by the treasurer upon warrant from the court or judge before whom the cause was tried and were to be added to the fines imposed upon conviction.[3]

Appeal was provided for in Liberty 36. The accused had to give security for his good behavior and appearance. It was added by a provision in the laws of 1660 and 1672 that "if the point of appeal" were "in the matter of Law," it should be decided by the bench; "if in the matter of fact, by the Bench and Jury."[4] As already noted, however, the General Court could take jurisdiction of any case upon petition.

No man was to be sentenced twice for the same offence;[5] and, as a rule, the death penalty was not to be executed within four days after it had been imposed.[6]

Besides grand and petty juries, there were coroner's juries. One of these was summoned as early as September 28, 1630.[7] It contained more than twelve men, but was limited later to that number, for Liberty 57 declared that in case of "any suddaine, untimely and unnaturall death, some assistant, or the constable of that Towne"

[1] *Mass. Col. Rec.*, vol. iv, pt. i, p. 291.

[2] Liberty 25; *Laws*, 1660–72, p. 124; *Laws*, 1672–86, p. 7.

[3] *Mass. Col. Rec.*, vol. ii, p. 205; *Laws*, 1660–72, p. 202; *Laws*, 1672–86, p. 159.

[4] *Laws*, 1660–72, p. 122; *Laws*, 1672–86, p. 3.

[5] Liberty 42; *Laws*, 1660–72, p. 187; *Laws*, 1672–86, p. 129.

[6] Liberty 44; *Laws*, 1660–72, p. 139; *Laws*, 1672–86, p. 30.

[7] *Mass. Col. Rec.*, vol. i, pp. 77–8; *Rec. Assist.*, vol. ii, pp. 6–7.

should "summon a jury of twelve freemen to" investigate "the cause and manner." Their verdict had to be presented to one of the magistrates or to the next court for that town.[1]

CRIMINAL LAW.

In dealing with crimes, the colonists went back in large measure to the Mosaic code. Here especially is Lechford's testimony in point:

I feare it is not a little degree of pride and dangerous improvidence to slight all former lawes of the Church or State, cases of experience and precedents, to go hammer out new, according to severall exegencies; upon the pretence that the Word of God is sufficient to rule us: It is true, it is sufficient, if well understood.[2]

Indictments usually read as follows: Such a one, being presented by the Grand Jury, was indicted by such a name, "for that he, not having the fear of God before his eyes & being instigated by the devill," on a certain day did commit a certain crime, "contrary to the peace of our Soveraigne Lord the king his Crowne & dignity the lawes of God & of this Jurisdiction."[3]

The tendency to adopt Mosaic law is especially marked in the conception of capital offenses. As early as 1631 adultery, the woman being married, was made a death crime.[4] But in 1637,[5] in place of this penalty, three adulterers were whipped and banished and charged never

[1] *Laws*, 1660–72, p. 145; *Laws*, 1672–86, p. 39.

[2] *Plain Dealing*, pp. 85–6.

[3] Cases in *Rec. Assist.*, vol. i.

[4] *Mass. Col. Rec.*, vol. i, p. 92.

[5] *Mass. Col. Rec.*, vol. i, pp. 198, 202–3, 225; Davis, *The Law of Adultery and Ignominious Punishments* (Worcester, Mass., 1895), p. 9.

to return on pain of death.[1] This was on the ground that the statute might not be valid, being made by the court of assistants with permission of the General Court, and might not have been sufficiently published. But the law of 1631 was immediately ratified[2] and remained in force until superseded by a like provision in the *Body of Liberties*.[3]

This brings us down to the *Body of Liberties*, and it will be more convenient to treat separately hereafter the statutes and decisions.

The capital offenses were set forth in Liberty 94. They included idolatry, witchcraft, blasphemy, premeditated murder, killing in anger, fatal poisoning and the like, bestiality,[4] sodomy,[5] adultery,[6] "man-stealing," perjury in capital cases, rebellion and treason. To these was added, in 1642, the rape of a woman either married or betrothed; but the rape of a single woman or maid over ten was to be punished by death or some other grievous punishment at the discretion of the judges. A child under ten could not give consent, and death was the

[1] *Mass. Col. Rec.*, vol. i, p. 225; Winthrop (Savage), vol. i, p. 309.

[2] *Mass. Col. Rec.*, vol. i, p. 225, Winthrop (Savage), vol. i, p. 309; Davis, p. 9; Howard, *A History of Matrimonial Institutions* (Chicago, 1904), vol. ii, p. 170.

[3] October 7, 1640, the following order was passed: "The first law against adultery, made by the Court of Assistants, Anno 1631, is declared to bee abrogated; but the other, made the first mo. 1637/8, by the General Court, to stand in force." *Mass. Col. Rec.*, vol. i, p. 301.

[4] "And the beast shall be slaine and buried and not eaten." Liberty 94; *Laws*, 1660–72, p. 128; *Laws*, 1672–86, p. 14. *Cf.* Leviticus 20, 15, 16.

[5] In the revisions, "unless the one partie were forced, or be under fourteen years of age in which case he shall be severely punished." *Laws*, 1660–72, p. 128; *Laws*, 1672–86, p. 15.

[6] "With a married or espoused wife," here and in the revisions.

punishment.[1] By laws passed in 1642 and 1647, burglary and highway robbery were made capital crimes upon the third conviction.[2] The return of a Jesuit after banishment was added in 1647.[3] And by order of 1652 the second conviction of denying the word of God was to be punished by death or banishment at the discretion of the court.[4] During the same year arson in case of a dwelling, church or store was added to the capital offenses, and the party convicted was to forfeit in addition so much of his lands, goods or chattels as to pay the loss.[5] By act of 1658 the return of Quakers was made a death crime.[6]

These laws were incorporated in the revision of 1660, with the addition of cursing or smiting parents by children over sixteen and being a rebellious son above the same age.[7] The law of 1642, making it a death crime to have carnal knowledge of a child under ten, was not included; but in a case in which the child was eight years old the General Court declared in 1669, in answer to a question, that carnal knowledge of a girl under ten should be a death crime.[8]

All the above capital laws were re-enacted in the revision of 1672.[9] Piracy and mutiny were added in 1673,[10] and treason against the king was defined and made a

[1] *Mass. Col. Rec.*, vol. ii, p. 21.

[2] *Laws*, 1660–72, p. 127.

[3] *Mass. Col. Rec.*, vol. ii, p. 193.

[4] *Ibid.*, vol. iv, pt. i, p. 78.

[5] *Ibid.*, vol. iv, pt. i, p. 83.

[6] *Ibid.*, vol. iv, pt. i, p. 346.

[7] *Laws*, 1660–72, pp. 127–9, 152, 154, 156, 158.

[8] *Mass. Col. Rec.*, vol. iv, pt. ii, p. 437.

[9] *Laws*, 1672–86, pp. 13–15, 52, 60, 61.

[10] *Mass. Col. Rec.*, vol. iv, pt. ii, p. 563; *Laws*, 1672–86, p. 211.

death crime in 1678.[1] The law making rebellious sons amenable to the death sentence was repealed in 1681, and at the same time a slight change was made in the wording of the law punishing treason against the colony.[2] What amounted to an addition to the law of treason against the king was passed in 1684, making military service against the king or his allies a death crime.[3]

When occasion arose, the death sentence was imposed by the courts. In 1643 James Britton and Mary Latham were sentenced to death for adultery.[4] Cotton Mather mentions the execution of an adulterer from Weymouth.[5] Several convictions for rape are found in the records. An Indian was sentenced in 1647 for the rape of another Indian's wife,[6] and a white man for the crime against another's wife in 1675.[7] In a case of 1676 the victim was a child about three years old, and the criminal a negro.[8] A master was sentenced to be hanged in 1681 for raping his servant.[9] In 1673 there was a conviction for bestiality; the mare was to be knocked in the head before the eyes of the sentenced person,[10] and then he was to be hanged.[11]

[1] *Mass. Col. Rec.*, vol. v, p. 194.

[2] *Laws*, 1672-86, p. 291.

[3] *Ibid.*, p. 315.

[4] *Rec. Assist.*, vol. i, p. 139; Winthrop (Savage), vol. ii, pp. 190-1; Howard, vol, ii, p. 170; Davis, p. 13.

[5] Mather, *Magnalia* (Hartford, 1820), vol. ii, p. 348.

[6] Case of Tom, Indian, *Rec. Assist.*, vol. i, p. 22.

[7] Case of Samuel Guile, *ibid.*, vol. i, p. 50.

[8] Case of Basto, Negro, *ibid.*, vol. i, p. 74.

[9] Case of Wm. Chany, *ibid.*, vol. i, p. 199.

[10] *Cf. supra*, p. 94, note 4.

[11] Case of Benj. Goad, *ibid.*, vol. i, p. 11.

The death sentence was imposed upon a girl in 1646 for killing her bastard child. In this case conviction was secured, first, by the superstitious test of touching the corpse and, second, by the confession of the accused.[1] Two servants were sentenced to be hanged in 1674 for the murder of their master;[2] and a like sentence was imposed upon a number of men in 1676 for killing Indian women and children.[3] In 1656 a woman was convicted of witchcraft and sentenced to be hanged.[4] There was another conviction for witchcraft in 1679, but the sentence is omitted in the records.[5] In 1681 there were two convictions for arson. The execution in one case was to be by burning,[6] and in the other case by hanging.[7] Piracy and treason cases also came before the courts. In 1675 Peter Rodriego and his confederates were sentenced to death for piracy;[8] and in 1676 a number of Indians received a like sentence for treason.[9]

The court seems to have hesitated at times in pronouncing the death sentence, substituting other severe punishments in its place. In 1677 a man accused of treason put himself upon trial by the bench. He was found guilty, but, in place of the death penalty, he was sentenced to run the gauntlet, forfeit all his lands and be

[1] Winthrop (Savage), vol. ii, pp. 368–70.

[2] *Rec. Assist.*, vol. i, pp. 30, 32.

[3] *Ibid.*, vol. i, pp. 71–3.

[4] Case of Ann Hibbins, *Mass. Col. Rec.*, vol. iv, pt. i, p. 269. This case was brought up to the General Court upon disagreement between bench and jury.

[5] Case of Elizabeth Morse, *Rec. Assist.*, vol. i, p. 159.

[6] Case of Maria, Negress, *ibid.*, vol. i, p. 198.

[7] Case of Jock, Negro, *ibid.*, vol. i, p. 199.

[8] *Ibid.*, vol. i, pp. 35–9.

[9] Case of Caleb and other Indians, *ibid.*, vol. i, p. 76.

banished upon pain of perpetual imprisonment.[1] Again, in 1678, a woman was convicted of unchastity and of having a bastard child while her husband was absent. She was sentenced to receive thirty-nine stripes at the cart's tail, pay the costs and leave Boston.[2]

Although the law prescribed the death penalty for the crimes already mentioned, the mode of execution was left for the courts to determine. Hanging was the usual method, but, as noted above, there was one execution by burning. In comparison to the number of capital trials there were few convictions.

The lesser crimes included, in general, offenses against the person; offenses against public morals and general welfare; offenses against religion; offenses against property; and offenses against the government. Here again the statutes and decisions will be separated in the discussion.

Laws punishing offenses against the person were not numerous. A statute of 1645 provided that lying should be punished by fine, stocks or whipping, according to whether it were the first offense or had been repeated several times.[3] A law of 1649 forbade malpractice by physicians and midwives, but did not attach any penalty.[4] This was probably left to the discretion of the court. A law of 1668 declared that a person breaking the peace by beating, hurting or striking another should pay damages to the injured or a fine to the country, or both, at

[1] Case of Walter Gendall, *Rec. Assist.*, vol. i, p. 102.

[2] Case of Ellinor May, *ibid.*, vol. i, p. 138.

[3] *Mass. Col. Rec.*, vol. ii, pp. 104-5; *Laws*, 1660-72, p. 171; *Laws*, 1672-86, pp. 91-2.

[4] *Mass. Col. Rec.*, vol. ii, pp. 278-9; *Laws*, 1660-72, pp. 137-8; *Laws*, 1672-86, p. 28.

the discretion of the court.[1] It was declared in 1678 that those who killed or wounded others by the careless or unlawful shooting of guns should be proceeded against as murderers and be liable for damage to the parties injured and amenable to such punishment as the court should impose.[2]

The punishments prescribed for offenses against public morals and general welfare were more numerous. By statute of 1633 idleness was to be punished at the discretion of the court.[3] An order of 1668 declared that those who neglected their families should be subject to the laws against idlers.[4] According to a statute of 1642 fornication was to be punished by enjoining marriage, by fine, by corporal punishment, or by all of these if the court saw fit.[5] It was added in 1665 that freemen could be disfranchised for the crime.[6] A further provision of 1668 required the reputed father to maintain the bastard child.[7] According to a statute of 1672, whoredom and maintaining houses of ill-fame were to be punished by whipping at the cart's tail and hard labor in the house of correction. Other disgraceful punishments were to be imposed upon bawds and their confederates.[8] Plurality

[1] *Mass. Col. Rec.*, vol. iv, pt. ii, p. 397; *Laws*, 1672–86, p. 11.

[2] *Laws*, 1672–86, p. 349.

[3] *Mass. Col. Rec.*, vol. i, p. 109; *Laws*, 1660–72, p. 158; *Laws*, 1672–86, p. 66.

[4] *Mass. Col. Rec.*, vol. iv, pt. ii, p. 395; *Laws*, 1660–72, p. 259; *Laws*, 1672–86, p. 66.

[5] *Mass. Col. Rec.*, vol. ii, p. 21; *Laws*, 1660–72, p. 153; *Laws*, 1672–86, p. 54.

[6] *Mass. Col. Rec.*, vol. iv, pt. ii, p. 143; *Laws*, 1660–72, p. 231; *Laws*, 1672–86, p. 55.

[7] *Mass. Col. Rec.*, vol. iv, p. ii, pp. 393–4; *Laws*, 1660–72, p. 257; *Laws*, 1672–86, p. 55.

[8] *Laws*, 1672–86, p. 208.

of husbands or wives was forbidden in 1647,[1] and marriage with a dead wife's sister in 1670.[2]

Common barratry, *i. e.* fomenting controversies, was made punishable by Liberty 34.[3] Scolds were not tolerated: it was declared in 1672 that they should be gagged or dipped three times in the ducking stool.[4]

Profane swearing was made punishable by a provision in the statutes of 1660 and 1672,[5] and it was added in 1675 that a person who heard profane oaths should be required to report the same under penalty of being punished as severely as the principal.[6]

As to religion, the statutes against heresy are too numerous to mention. A law of 1646 made certain unorthodox teachings finable,[7] and in the same year Christians who interrupted the minister were made subject to censure and humiliating punishment.[8] The long list of statutes against the Anabaptists and Quakers need not be catalogued here. Laws enjoining the observance of the Sabbath go back to an early date,[9] but the first positive act making it a crime, punishable by fine or whipping, to profane the day, was passed in 1653.[10] This provision

[1] *Mass. Col. Rec.*, vol. ii, p. 212; *Laws*, 1660–72, p. 172; *Laws*, 1672–86, p. 101.

[2] *Mass. Col. Rec.*, vol. iv, pt. ii, p. 454; *Laws*, 1672–86, p. 102.

[3] *Laws*, 1660–72, p. 125; *Laws*, 1672–86, p. 9.

[4] *Laws*, 1672–86, p. 206.

[5] *Laws*, 1660–72, p. 194; *Laws*, 1672–86, p. 145.

[6] *Laws*, 1672–86, p. 235.

[7] *Mass. Col. Rec.*, vol. ii, p. 177; *Laws*, 1660–72, p. 154; *Laws*, 1672–86, p. 59.

[8] *Mass. Col. Rec.*, vol. ii, p. 179; Davis. p. 21.

[9] *Mass. Col. Rec.*, vol. i, p. 395.

[10] *Ibid.*, vol. iv, pt. i, pp. 150–1; *Laws*, 1660–72, p. 189; *Laws*, 1672–86, pp. 132–3.

was extended in 1658 to Saturday and Sunday nights.[1] The Sabbath laws were strengthened by order of 1665, which made neglect or refusal to submit to sentence in such matters contempt of court and corporally punishable.[2] It was added in 1668 that persons doing work, except that of piety, charity, or necessity, on the Sabbath should be fined, and the same penalty was to be imposed for Sunday travel.[3]

There was, of course, much legislation regarding offenses against property. Burglary and highway robbery, according to a law of 1642, were to be severely punished.[4] In the matter of burglary, no distinction was made between day and night. By the revision of 1660 and 1672, the punishment for these crimes, if committed on secular days, was branding "on the forehead with the letter (B)" for the first offense and branding and whipping for the second offense. If they were committed on the Sabbath day, then, besides the above punishment, one ear was to be cut off for the first offense and the other ear for the second offense. The third offense in either case, as already noted, was a death crime.[5] For ordinary theft the statutes of 1646 and 1652 established various penalties, such as restitution up to threefold, fine or whipping according to the circumstances of the case.[6]

Embezzlement by a servant or workman was made

[1] *Mass. Col. Rec.*, vol. iv, pt. i, p. 347; *Laws*, 1660–72, p. 190; *Laws*, 1672–86, p. 133.

[2] *Laws*, 1660–72, p. 232; *Laws*, 1672–86, p. 133.

[3] *Mass. Col. Rec.*, vol. iv, pt. ii, p. 395; *Laws*, 1660–72, p. 259; *Laws*, 1672–86, p. 134.

[4] *Mass. Col. Rec.*, vol. ii, p. 22.

[5] *Laws*, 1660–72, p. 127; *Laws*, 1672–86, pp. 12–13.

[6] *Mass. Col. Rec.*, vol. ii, p. 180; vol. iv, pt. i, p. 82; *Laws*, 1660–72, pp. 127–8; *Laws*, 1672–86, pp. 13–14.

punishable in 1646,[1] and by an executor or administrator in 1649.[2] The penalty prescribed for forgery in 1646 was standing in the pillory three lecture days, double restitution and disqualification for service as a witness or juryman.[3] It was ordered in 1652 that arson in case of a stable, mill, outhouse, stack of wood, corn or hay, or anything of like nature, should be punished by imposing double damage and whipping.[4]

The earliest legislation regarding offenses against government imposed penalties for failure to support law and order. An act was passed in 1646, to the effect that if any officer or other person should refuse to put forth his best effort "in raising & prosecuting hue and crys by foote & if neede be, by horse, after such as" had "committed capitall crymes," he should "forfeite, for every offense, to the common treasury, forty shillings."[5] In order to escape public service, some of the church members had not applied for admission as freemen; but according to the revisions church members were required to serve as constables, jurymen, selectmen, and surveyors of highways, and refusal was to be punished by fine.[6] Contempt of authority and resistance to legal process were of course penalized. Defamation of courts or magistrates was punishable by whipping, fine, im-

[1] *Mass. Col. Rec.*, vol. ii, p. 180; *Laws*, 1660–72, p. 127; *Laws*, 1672–86, p. 13.

[2] *Mass. Col. Rec.*, vol. ii, p. 287; *Laws*, 1660–72, p. 201; *Laws*, 1672–86, p. 167.

[3] *Mass. Col. Rec.*, vol. ii, p. 181; *Laws*, 1660–72, p. 153; *Laws*, 1672–86, p. 54.

[4] *Mass. Col. Rec.*, vol. iv, pt. i, p. 83; *Laws*, 1660–72, p. 152; *Laws*, 1672–86, p. 52.

[5] *Mass. Col. Rec.*, vol. ii, p. 182; *Laws*, 1660–72, p. 140; *Laws*, 1672–86, p. 31.

[6] *Laws*, 1660–72, p. 153; *Laws*, 1672–86, p. 55.

prisonment, disfranchisement or banishment, according to the circumstances.[1] It was declared in 1668 that a person who had lost his title to house or land through a judgment in court and retained forcible possession after execution had been served should "be counted a high offender against the law, & breaker of the publick peace" and fined or punished in some other way as the case required.[2] A statute of 1669 made a person who secured the escape of another from prison liable to the same penalty as the one he assisted, and to fine, corporal punishment or imprisonment in addition, if the court saw fit.[3]

Turning to the decisions, it will be found that the statutes were supplemented as well as enforced. Even in the matters covered by the laws a great deal of discretion was left to the court, and such power was freely exercised.

The same general outline will be followed as in discussing the statutes, *viz:* offenses against the person; offenses against public morals, and general welfare; offenses against religion; offences against property; and offenses against the government.

For libel, a fine was imposed in 1637,[4] but for slander the punishment in 1640 amounted only to an acknowledgment to the person injured.[5] The same year a fine was imposed for rude and contemptuous speeches.[6] In 1675 an Indian was to receive thirty-nine stripes for

[1] *Laws*, 1660–72, p. 153; *Laws*, 1672–86, p. 36.

[2] *Mass. Col. Rec.*, vol. iv, pt. ii, p. 397; *Laws*, 1672–86, p. 11.

[3] *Mass. Col. Rec.*, vol. iv, pt. ii, p. 423; *Laws*, 1672–86, p. 129.

[4] Case of Angell Holland, *Rec. Assist.*, vol. ii, p. 72.

[5] Case of Nathaniel Travell, *ibid.*, vol. ii, p. 93.

[6] Case of Walter Night, *ibid.*, vol. ii, p. 104.

abusive speech.[1] For writing untruths in a letter, the punishment in 1675 was to be damage to the party wronged and a fine to the country.[2] The offense of attacking the chastity of women was considered especially heinous: in 1677 a person convicted of defaming the character of a woman was ordered to stand upon the gallows for an hour with a rope about his neck, to receive thirty-nine stripes and to pay the costs.[3] Attempts to commit certain crimes were punished. In 1638 the penalty for an attempt to rape was, in addition to five pounds to be paid the maid, whipping and imprisonment.[4] In 1642 a woman was sentenced to be whipped and kept at hard labor and on spare diet for trying to drown her child.[5] Cases of assault and battery early occupied the attention of the court. In 1631 a servant was ordered to be whipped for striking a person who came to correct him for idleness in his master's work.[6] A man was fined in 1641 for striking another man.[7] Where one person killed another with kicks and blows, probably after a quarrel, the court's sentence in 1683 was burning in the hand and forfeiture of possessions.[8] As to criminal negligence, the penalty imposed in 1675 for accidentally shooting and killing a boy was damage and fine.[9] The same year there was a like penalty for driving over and killing

[1] Case of Old Jethro, Indian, *Rec. Assist.*, vol. i, p. 54.

[2] Case of Richard Scott, *ibid.*, vol. i, p. 61.

[3] Case of Ephraim Beamis, *ibid.*, vol. i, p. 116.

[4] Case of Thomas Boyse, *ibid.*, vol. ii, p. 81.

[5] Case of Anne Hett, *ibid.*, vol. ii, p. 126.

[6] Case of John Legge, *ibid.*, vol. ii, p. 14.

[7] Case of Symon Voysey, *ibid.*, vol. ii, p. 115.

[8] Case of Leonard Pomery, *ibid.*, vol. i, pp. 242-3.

[9] Case of John Foster, *ibid.*, vol. i, p. 54.

a child.[1] Where a person killed another at night by accidental shooting, he was required in 1677 to pay a fine and damage.[2] A similar offense was punished in 1680 by imposing damage and costs.[3]

On the subject of public morals and general welfare there was a large number of cases. Fornication was punished by whipping in 1632.[4] Whipping was usually imposed; but, in 1639, for seducing and refusing to marry the girl, the man was committed to prison until he should give sufficient security to provide for the mother and child or make up his mind for the marriage.[5] In 1641, for the "ravage" of a girl, in addition to the whipping, the girl's father was to be paid twenty pounds.[6] A similar case came up in 1642, and, besides the whipping, a sum of five pounds was to be paid the master of two ravaged girls.[7] The statute of 1642 enjoined marriage, but this could not be enforced in all cases, especially if the man already had a wife. In 1643 a married man was fined for the offense twenty pounds, half of which was to go toward bringing up the child and the remainder to the public treasury.[8] The penalty imposed in 1680 was fine and provision for the child.[9] The statute requiring the reputed father to maintain the child was usually enforced. In 1683 a woman was punished by whipping

[1] Case of James Foorde, *ibid.*, vol. i, p. 60.

[2] Case of Samuel Hunting, *ibid.*, vol. i, p. 114.

[3] Case of Jno. Dyre, *ibid.*, vol. i, p. 188.

[4] Case of Robert Huitt and Mary Ridge, *ibid.*, vol. ii, p. 30.

[5] Case of John Vaughn, *ibid.*, vol. ii, p. 91.

[6] Case of Jonathan Thing, *ibid.*, vol. ii, p. 106.

[7] Case of Robt. Wyar and Jno. Garland, *ibid.*, vol. ii, p. 121.

[8] Case of Wm. Flint, *ibid.*, vol. ii, p. 137.

[9] Case of Geo. Russel, *ibid.*, vol. i, p. 169.

and costs of trial.[1] The court punished even husbands and wives for fornication before marriage. A couple were fined for this offense in 1635.[2] A fine was the usual punishment, but in 1642 a husband and wife were ordered to stand an hour in the market place with great letters on their hats.[3] For fornication as well as for many other offenses, humiliating punishment was often inflicted.

A case of polygamy came up in 1639. A man having a wife in England had married again in the colony. His last marriage was declared void; all his property was to be given to his last wife and her children, and he was sentenced to be set in the stocks one hour and then to be sent to England at the earliest opportunity.[4] Another case of polygamy was brought before the court of assistants in March, 1643, but was taken to the General Court, where decision was rendered the following November. The last marriage was declared void, but the penalty is not stated.[5]

Minor cases of unchaste behavior did not escape notice. In 1638 the penalty imposed for attempting lewdness with women was whipping and wearing a large letter "V."[6] At the same court, a fine and the payment of a sum to two maids was prescribed for enticing them.[7] For a similar offense, the sentence in 1639 was whipping and commitment as a slave to a party

[1] Case of Elizabeth Payne, *Rec. Assist.*, vol. i, p. 228.

[2] Case of Edward Gyles, *etc.*, *ibid.*, vol. ii, p. 60.

[3] Case of Thomas Scot and wife, *ibid.*, vol. ii, p. 124.

[4] Case of James Luxford, *ibid.*, vol. ii, p. 89.

[5] Case of John Richardson, *ibid.*, vol. ii, p. 139; *Mass. Col. Rec.*, vol. ii, p. 86.

[6] Case of John Davies, *Rec. Assist.*, vol. ii, p. 81.

[7] Case of Richard Ibrooke, *ibid.*

designated by the court.[1] Where the woman was a wife, such behavior was called adulterous. In 1645 a couple were sentenced, for conduct which tended to adultery, to stand upon the ladder at the place of execution one hour with halters about their necks and then be whipped or pay twenty pounds apiece.[2] For adulterous carriage a woman was ordered in 1673 to stand one hour in the market place wearing an inscription, and then to receive thirty stripes.[3] In 1683, a like punishment was imposed upon a couple, with the addition of costs.[4]

Attempts to commit capital crimes of an immoral nature were severely punished. A case of attempted bestiality was before the court in 1642: the penalty imposed upon the culprit was to stand in the place of execution with a halter about the neck and to receive a severe whipping.[5]

Cheating and lying were punished in various ways. In 1630 the penalty imposed for selling worthless medicine at a high price was either fine or whipping;[6] in 1638, for taking above double toll a fine;[7] and in 1639, for cheating, restitution and whipping.[8] For a false oath the penalty imposed in 1674 was either ten stripes or forty shillings' costs.[9]

For idleness a fine was imposed in 1639 and whipping

[1] Case of John Kempe, *ibid.*, vol. ii, p. 86.

[2] Winthrop (Savage), vol. ii, pp. 105-6.

[3] Case of Ruth Read, *Rec. Assist.*, vol. i, p. 10.

[4] Case of Joshua Rice and Elizabeth Crocket, *ibid.*, vol. i, p. 240.

[5] Case of T. Ocrimi, *ibid.*, vol. ii, p. 121.

[6] Case of Rich. Knopp, *ibid.*, vol. ii, p. 11.

[7] Case of Thomas Wilson, *ibid.*, vol. ii, p. 78.

[8] Case of Richard Joanes, *ibid.*, vol. ii, p. 88.

[9] Case of Edward Thomson, *ibid.*, vol. i, p. 24.

in 1642, but both of these cases were aggravated by other misconduct.[1]

Drunkenness and swearing early occupied the attention of the courts, and the convictions for these offenses were almost numberless. In 1632 a fine was imposed for drunkenness.[2] In 1633 the punishment decreed was setting in the bilboes,[3] and in 1636 whipping was ordered.[4] These were the usual punishments for drinking to excess or in forbidden places or at forbidden times. For cursing and swearing the penalty imposed in 1632 was whipping;[5] in 1634 it was the bilboes;[6] and in 1636 the condemned was sentenced to have his tongue placed in a cleft stick and thus to remain for a half-hour.[7] In 1642 a fine[8] was imposed for swearing; and these, or a combination of them, constituted the punishments for this offense.

There were numerous convictions for offenses against religion. "Remember the Sabbath day to keep it holy" was never out of the mind of the Puritan judge. As early as 1630 a man was sentenced to be whipped for shooting at fowl on Sunday,[9] and in 1638 traveling on the Lord's day was punished by setting the culprit in the stocks.[10] Banishment on pain of death was the punish-

[1] *Rec. Assist.*, pp. 84, 126.

[2] Case of James Parker, *ibid.*, vol. ii, p. 25.

[3] Case of Wm. Dixon, *ibid.*, vol. ii, p. 32.

[4] Case of John Whitele, *ibid.*, vol. ii, p. 63.

[5] Case of Robert Shawe, *ibid.*, vol. ii, p. 26.

[6] Case of Henry Bright, *ibid.*, vol. ii, p. 50.

[7] Case of Robt. Shorthose, *ibid.*, vol. ii, p. 63.

[8] Case of George Watts, *ibid.*, vol. ii, p. 127.

[9] Case of John Baker, *ibid.*, vol. i, p. 9.

[10] Case of Richard Hollingsworth, *ibid.*, vol. ii, p. 80.

ment for heresy in 1640,[1] and whipping for dishonoring the name of God in 1641.[2] Fifteen stripes were prescribed in 1678 for disturbing worship.[3]

The punishments imposed for offenses against property were various. In 1643 whipping and binding out to service were ordered for breaking into houses and stealing articles.[4] In 1630 stealing a loaf of bread was punished by whipping.[5] In 1633, for an aggravated case of theft, the sentence was whipping, double restitution, forfeiture of the remainder of the estate and binding to service for three years.[6] A similar offense was punished in 1635 by setting the culprit in the bilboes and then requiring him to move from his home town;[7] in 1638, by a fine alone.[8] Humiliating punishments were often added to the others. Besides an alternative between a fine and being bound to service, the condemned was sentenced in 1639 to wear a large letter "T."[9] Restitution was frequently required. In 1679 the punishment was treble restitution and ten stripes,[10] and in 1680 treble restitution and banishment on pain of death.[11] These, or a combination of them, seem to have been the usual punishments for theft. Abettors and accomplices in theft did not escape the hand of justice. Receiving stolen wine was punished in 1643 by

[1] Case of Hugh Buett, *ibid.*, vol. ii, p. 101.

[2] Case of the wife of Robt. Lewis, *ibid.*, vol. ii, p. 106.

[3] Case of Alexander Colman, *ibid.*, vol. ii, p. 127.

[4] Case of Nathaniel Toppin, *ibid.*, vol. ii, p. 132.

[5] Case of Bartholomew Hill, *ibid.*, vol. ii, p. 9.

[6] Case of John Sayle, *ibid.*, vol. ii, p. 32.

[7] Case of Griffin Montague, *ibid.*, vol. ii, p. 53.

[8] Case of Isaack Deersbury, *ibid.*, vol. ii, p. 81.

[9] Case of Richard Wilson, *ibid.*, vol. ii, p. 86.

[10] Case of Sara Bradbrooke, *ibid.*, vol. i, p. 145.

[11] Case of Tho. Davis and Jno. Eggerton, *ibid.*, vol. i, p. 189.

damage and fine.[1] The penalty imposed in 1679 for inciting others to steal a boat and turn pirate was fifteen stripes and costs.[2] Arson, where a servant fired the barn of his master, was punished in 1640 by binding the culprit to the service of his master for twenty-one years.[3]

Among the offenses against the government were words spoken against officers, laws or courts, and defiance of authority. As early as 1630 whipping was imposed for intimating that the court had taken a bribe.[4] For speaking against the government and churches a man was sentenced in 1631 to be whipped, to have his ears cut off and to be banished.[5] Setting in the bilboes was the penalty in 1632 for threatening to have the court tried in England,[6] and a fine in 1634 for charging the court with injustice.[7] Every portion of the machinery of justice was carefully guarded. In 1640 a man "was bound to his good behavior & fined" for saying: "Shall I pay 12^d for the fragments which the grand jury roages have left?"[8] Contempt of court was punished in 1675 by requiring the culprit to stand an hour with one ear nailed to the pillory and then to be released by having it cut off.[9] An appellant who held a colonial office was deprived of his office and fined one hundred pounds in 1677 for casting reflections upon the honor of a county court

[1] Case of Robt. Rogers, *Rec. Assist.*, vol. ii, p. 131.
[2] Case of Morris Conway, *ibid.*, vol. i, p. 144.
[3] Case of Henry Stevens, *ibid.*, vol. ii, p. 100.
[4] Case of Tho. Foxe, *ibid.*, vol. ii, p. 12.
[5] Case of Phillip Ratcliffe, *ibid.*, vol. ii, p. 16.
[6] Case of Tho. Knower, *ibid.*, vol. ii, p. 21.
[7] Case of Ensigne Jennison, *ibid.*, vol. ii, p. 48.
[8] Case of Richard Cluffe, *ibid.*, vol. ii, p. 97.
[9] Case of Maurice Brett, *ibid.*, vol. i, p. 57.

in his reasons for appeal.[1] The integrity of the ministry was not left without protection. A case in point came up in 1639, when "Samuel Norman was Committed for want of security, & was censured to be whipped, for saying 'if ministers which come will but raile against England some would receive them.'"[2]

Punishment was visited upon those who thwarted justice or attempted to influence unduly judge or jury. Thomas Lechford was disbarred in 1639 for pleading with the jury out of court;[3] and in 1675 a juryman was fined ten pounds "for his contemptuous carriage in the Court in obstructing the eleven of the jury dissenting from them from time to time & not Giving the Court a satisfactory Reason."[4] Absence from or refusal to serve on juries was punishable. A fine of ten shillings was imposed for absence from a petty jury in 1633[5], and in 1638 a fine of five shillings for not serving on the grand jury.[6] Fine was the usual penalty. When it came to escape from justice, the court was more stringent. The alternative between a fine of twenty pounds and a severe whipping was imposed in 1641 for prison-breach,[7] and a like penalty in 1677 for assisting a prisoner to escape. In the latter case the fine of twenty pounds was reduced upon petition "to forty shillings & fees of Court," which were promptly paid.[8]

[1] Case of Capt. Bratles, *ibid.*, vol. i, p. 103.

[2] *Ibid.*, vol. ii, p. 82.

[3] *Ibid.*, vol. ii, p. 87.

[4] Case of Jacob Jesson, *ibid.*, vol. i, p. 55.

[5] Case of Mr. Palmer, *ibid.*, vol. ii, p. 35.

[6] Case of Henry Collens, *ibid.*, vol. ii, p. 76.

[7] Case of Thomas Owen, *ibid.*, vol. ii, p. 109.

[8] Case of Robert Dendy, *ibid.*, vol. i, pp. 115-6.

TORTS

Private wrongs were closely connected with public wrongs, and the colonists drew no fine distinctions between the two. As has been already noted, a private claim or right was often recognized in a criminal case, *viz.*, where a fine was divided between an injured party and the public treasury. Although not distinctly separated from criminal law, torts were yet penalized, and recognition of torts is to be found alike in the statutes and in the decisions. Here, as in the discussion of crimes, the statutes and decisions will be treated separately.

Malicious prosecution was discouraged. Liberty 22 declared that, if any man should falsely pretend great debts or damages in order to vex his adversary in a suit, the court could set a reasonable fine on his head. By Liberty 37 the court had power to assess damages against a plaintiff for wrongful prosecution. These provisions were combined in the later revisions, with the addition that there should be treble damages and a fine of forty shillings in such vexatious prosecutions. It was also provided that where the plaintiff claimed above forty shillings, and it was found to be less on the hearing, he should lose his action and pay the costs.[1]

Remedies were provided for damage done to property. By an order of 1646, anyone who purposely destroyed by fire or other means "any frame timber hewed, heaps or stacks of woode, coales, corne, hay, strawe, hemp, or flax" should "restore double damage to the owner."[2] And by another order of the same date, persons were made liable for all damage done by the fires they kindled

[1] *Laws*, 1660–72, p. 122; *Laws*, 1672–86, p. 3.

[2] *Mass. Col. Rec.*, vol. ii, p. 180; *Laws*, 1660–72, p. 151; *Laws*, 1672–86, p. 51.

in the woods, except during the period between the tenth of March and the last of April, exclusive of all intervening Saturdays and Sundays. On the criminal side there was to be a fine equal to half the damage.[1] The compensation provided in the statute of 1652 for loss by arson has already been noted in discussing crimes: in case of a dwelling, church or store, the party convicted was to forfeit so much of his lands, goods or chattels as to pay the loss; in case of a stable, mill, outhouse, stack of wood, corn or hay, or anything of like nature, there were to be double damages.[2] It was ordered in 1646 that any one committing forgery should, besides the criminal penalty, render the party wronged double damage.[3] Two other orders of the same date are worthy of mention. The first required servants and workingmen to make restitution for goods taken from their masters and employers, and the second required treble restitution for theft in orchards or gardens.[4]

In regard to negligence in keeping bridges and highways in repair, it was enacted in 1647 that, after due warning that a bridge or highway was in bad condition, if any person lost his life through such defect, the county or town responsible should pay a "fine" of one hundred pounds to the parents, husband, wife, children or next of kin. In case a person had been injured only, he was to receive double damages. Like satisfaction was to be

[1] *Mass. Col. Rec.*, vol. ii, p. 180; *Laws*, 1660-72, p. 151; *Laws*, 1672-86, p. 51.

[2] *Mass. Col. Rec.*, vol. iv, pt. i, p. 83; *Laws*, 1660-72, p. 152; *Laws*, 1672-86, p. 52.

[3] *Mass. Col. Rec.*, vol. ii, p. 181; *Laws*, 1660-72, p. 153; *Laws*, 1672-86, p. 54.

[4] *Mass. Col. Rec.*, vol. ii, pp. 180-1; *Laws*, 1660-72, p. 127; *Laws*, 1672-86, p. 13.

made for injury to horses, teams, carts, carriages or other property.[1]

According to the revisions of 1660 and 1672,

> Every Inkeeper or victualler [had to] provide for the entertainment of strangers horses, viz: one or more inclosures, for summer, hay and Provender for winter, with convenient stable-roome and attendance, under the penalty of *two shillings six pence* for every dayes default, & double damage to the party thereby wronged, except it [were] by inevitable accident.[2]

In 1646 it was declared unlawfull for any person "either fisherman or other, either forreyner or of this country," to enter upon the land apportioned to a town or individual or to take wood or timber therefrom without the owner's permission. But fishermen employed by the inhabitants were to have certain privileges connected with their occupation, such as drying fish on land near the harbors and gathering firewood where it could be spared. The owner was to have due compensation for the latter.[3] This order, which discriminated against fishermen employed by foreigners, was repealed in 1661.[4] All the repeal accomplished was to take away the privileges granted to domestic fishermen and to make all persons equally subject to the action of trespass. But owing to a "Reservation in the Patent," privileges similar to those mentioned above were granted in 1668 to foreign

[1] *Mass. Col. Rec.*, vol. ii, pp. 228-9; *Laws*, 1660-72, pp. 126-7; *Laws*, 1672-86, p. 12.

[2] *Laws*, 1660-72, p. 165; *Laws*, 1672-86, p. 82.

[3] *Mass. Col. Rec.*, vol. ii, p. 147; *Laws*, 1660-72, p. 152; *Laws*, 1672-86, p. 52.

[4] *Mass. Col. Rec.*, vol. iv, pt. ii, p. 32; *Laws*, 1660-72, p. 220; *Laws*, 1672-86, p. 52.

fishermen. It was expressly stated that such privileges did not extend "to Fishermen that" were "Inhabitants"; these were "not to trespass upon any person in their property, but" were "liable to make satisfaction with damages as in any other Action of Trespass."[1] Although there was no direct statute upon the subject, it may be concluded, from the wording of the orders in regard to fishermen, that as a rule anyone who entered the land of another without permission was liable for damage.

Trespass by animals was the subject of many statutes. As early as 1631 it was declared that, for the year, the owners of cows, horses or goats, in any plantation except Salem, should be liable for damage done by them in trespassing upon the corn of another. According to the same provision, all swine found in any man's corn were to be forfeited to the public. The damage, however, had to be paid out of such swine, and, if they were not enough, the owner had to make up the deficiency in other property.[2] But by order of 1637, if swine were well ringed and yoked, there had to be breach of a lawful fence before the owner was liable.[3] A lawful fence, according to the revisions, was one considered sufficient against great cattle.[4]

The owner of cattle was not liable, according to an order of 1637, unless the fences were sufficient and the damage was done through the unruliness of the animals.[5] It was declared, in 1642, that where fields were fenced

[1] *Mass. Col. Rec.*, vol. iv, pt. ii, p. 368; *Laws*, 1660-72, p. 245; *Laws*, 1672-86, p. 53.

[2] *Mass. Col. Rec.*, vol. i, p. 86.

[3] *Ibid.*, vol. i, p. 215; *Laws*, 1660-72, p. 195; *Laws*, 1672-86, pp. 145-6.

[4] *Laws*, 1660-72, p. 195; *Laws*, 1672-86, pp. 145-6.

[5] *Mass. Col. Rec.*, vol. i, p. 221.

in common and cattle entered through a defective portion of the fence, the party owning that portion should be liable. In case this could not be shown, each of the parties was to be liable in proportion to the condition of his part of the fence. But if all the fence was sufficient, then the owner of the cattle was liable.[1] An order of 1647 required cattle to be branded and fields fenced; and if an animal not branded trespassed upon a field lawfully fenced, the animal's owner had to pay double damage.[2] The amount of compensation due for harm done by cattle and horses in fields lawfully fenced was fixed by arbitration, but the decision was subject to review in the courts.[3] According to the revisions of 1660 and 1672, injury done by goats required double recompense; and when any man found goats in his corn or garden, he could use them until full satisfaction was made by the owner.[4] The laws in regard to the trespass of cattle were not well understood. It was ordered, therefore, in 1662, that, when cattle trespassed upon property not sufficiently fenced against cows or against swine properly ringed and yoked, and when the fence viewers did not consider such cattle unruly, the owners of the animals should not be liable.[5]

Animals belonging to another were not to be molested or injured. A law of 1647 made a person who took and used another's "Horse, Mare, or drawing beast" without permission, liable for treble damage, or the sum of only ten shillings, if the complainant desired. Those

[1] *Mass. Col. Rec.*, vol. ii, pp. 14-15.

[2] *Exodus*, 22, 5 and 21, 36, is referred to as authority for this order.

[3] *Mass. Col. Rec.*, vol. ii, p. 190; *Laws*, 1660-72, pp. 130-1; *Laws*, 1672-86, p. 18.

[4] *Laws*, 1660-72, p. 131; *Laws*, 1672-86, pp. 18, 19.

[5] *Mass. Col. Rec.*, vol. iv, pt. ii, p. 42; *Laws*, 1672-86, p. 20.

unable to pay were to be criminally punished.[1] According to an order of 1648, persons who molested sheep, or kept dogs that killed or molested them, were required to pay double damages. There were to be penalties in addition, and sheep-killing dogs were to be hanged.[2]

Such were the statutes; let us now consider the decisions. Among the private wrongs recognized and redressed by the courts, were those closely connected with a man's person or family. In 1641, a father was to be paid twenty pounds for the seduction of his daughter;[3] and, in 1642, the master of the two seduced girls was to receive five pounds.[4] A case of battery was before the court in 1631, and damage was awarded.[5] Where abusive language had been written in a letter, the person wronged was granted, in 1675, one hundred pounds compensation.[6] Persons were protected against vexatious suits. In 1637, damages were awarded a defendant whom a plaintiff summoned to court but failed to prosecute;[7] and in 1640, in a similar case, costs were assessed against the plaintiff.[8]

Property rights were carefully guarded. Loss by theft required recompense. In 1631 double restitution was adjudged for corn stolen from the Indians.[9] This was

[1] *Mass. Col. Rec.*, vol. ii, p. 195; *Laws*, 1660–72, p. 131; *Laws*, 1672–86, p. 19. "Asse" added in these revisions.

[2] *Mass. Col. Rec.*, vol. ii, pp. 151-2; *Laws*, 1660–72, p. 191; *Laws*, 1672–86, p. 138.

[3] Case of Jonathan Thing, *Rec Assist.*, vol. ii, p. 106.

[4] Case of Robt. Wyar and Jno. Garland, *ibid.*, vol. ii, p. 121.

[5] Thomas Dexter against Capt. Endicott, *ibid.*, vol. ii, p. 15.

[6] Case of James Foord, *ibid.*, vol. i, p. 60.

[7] Sam. Freeman, *ibid.*, vol. ii, p. 72.

[8] George Richardson, *ibid.*, vol. ii, p. 101.

[9] Josias Plastowe, *ibid.*, vol. ii, p. 19.

the general rule,[1] but in 1680 there was an aggravated case in which treble damages were awarded.[2] A case of cheating came before the court in 1639, and the party convicted was "put to the assigne of the party wronged to make satisfaction for the money" he received and spent.[3] "For firing the barn of his master" a servant was ordered, in 1640, to remain with the owner twenty-one years "toward recompencing the losse."[4] Harm done by cattle in corn was to be paid for, in 1632, with a certain amount of corn.[5]

Private wrongs resulting from negligence were often before the courts. In 1675 a father was awarded ten pounds damage against a person who accidentally shot and killed his son;[6] in 1677 a wife was granted twenty pounds where her husband was killed under similar circumstances;[7] and in 1680 an Indian woman received six pounds for a like loss.[8] When a girl was killed, in 1684, by a gun carelessly discharged by another, the parents were awarded five pounds damage against the offender.[9]

CONTRACTS

There were three classes of contracts: (1) contracts of record, (2) contracts under seal, and (3) simple contracts. The best examples of contracts of record were bail in criminal and bond in civil cases.

[1] See other cases in *Rec. Assist.*, vol. ii.

[2] Case of Tho. Davis, *ibid.*, vol. i, p. 189. *Cf. ibid*, vol. i. p. 145.

[3] Case of Richard Joanes, *ibid.*, vol. ii, p. 88.

[4] Case of Henry Stevens, *ibid.*, vol. ii, p. 100.

[5] Damage granted Saggamore John, *ibid.*, vol. ii, p. 29.

[6] Case of John Foster, *ibid.*, vol. i, p. 54.

[7] Case of Peeter Bent, *ibid.*, vol. i, p. 86.

[8] Case of John Dyar, *ibid.*, vol. i, p. 188.

[9] Case of John Dounton, *ibid.*, vol. i, p. 272.

Contracts under seal followed the English form[1] and included both indentures and deeds-poll.[2] Like English deeds, they were sealed and delivered, but in addition they were signed,[3] and the signing and sealing took place in the presence of witnesses.[4] As will appear later, recording was also necessary for their validity.

Most of these elements were prescribed by various orders which were included in the revisions of 1660 and 1672. It was enacted, October 7, 1640, that

> no morgage, bargaine, sale, or grant hereafter to bee made of any houses, lands, rents, or other hereditaments[5] shall bee of force against any other person except the granter & his heirs, unless the same bee recorded, as is hereafter expressed: And that no such bargaine, sale, or grant already made in way of morgage, where the granter remaines in possession, shalbee of force against any other but the granter or his heirs, except the same shalbee entered, as is hereafter expressed, within one month after the end of this Courte, if the partye bee within this jurisdiction, or else within three months after hee shall return.

This act further declared that the grantor could be forced to acknowledge his grant in case the grantee demanded it, and it also prescribed the method of recording the above writings. Of course documents other than deeds were included, the purpose being to prevent

[1] See *Suffolk Deeds* (Boston, 1880–1906).

[2] See *Mass. Col. Rec.*, vol. v, and *Suffolk Deeds*.

[3] At common law, until the enactment of the Statute of Frauds, 1677, signing was unnecessary. Art. "Deeds," *American and English Encyclopedia of Law*.

[4] See *Suffolk Deeds*.

[5] "Where the granter remaines in possession" inserted in the revisions.

"all fraudulent conveyances" and to provide a means by which persons might know what interest others had in property in which they wished to deal.[1] Liberty 15 had already provided that fraudulent deeds or conveyances for the purpose of defeating any man's just claim were void; and Liberty 40 had declared that "no conveyance, deed or promise whatsoever" was valid if obtained under "Dures."[2] In addition to these provisions, the form which should be used "in all deeds and conveyances of houses and lands" was prescribed May 7, 1651.[3]

The functions and necessary elements of deeds were finally set forth October 19, 1652. After citing as precedent the method of conveying houses and lands in England, the Court ordered

> that henceforth no sale or alienation of houses or lands within this jurisdiction shalbee holden good in lawe, except the same be donne by deede, in writing, under hand and seale, and delivered and possession given upon parte, in the name of the whole by the seller, or his atturney, so authorized under hand and seale, & unless the said deede be acknowledged according to lawe, and recorded.[4]

Such was the law in regard to contracts under seal. The parties to such contracts had to be twenty-one years of age.[5] At first, however, this was not strictly true, for Liberty 14 had provided that a conveyance

[1] *Mass. Col. Rec.*, vol. i, pp. 306-7; *Laws*, 1660-72, pp. 140-1; *Laws*, 1672-86, p. 33.

[2] *Laws*, 1660-72, p. 140; *Laws*, 1672-86, p. 32.

[3] *Mass. Col. Rec.*, vol. iv, pt. i, p. 39; *Laws*, 1660-72, p. 140; *Laws*, 1672-86, p. 32.

[4] *Mass. Col. Rec.*, vol. iv, pt. i, p. 101; *Laws*, 1660-72, p. 140; *Laws*, 1672-86, p. 32.

[5] Liberty 53; *Laws*, 1660-72, p. 121; *Laws*, 1672-86, p. 1.

made by a married woman, a child, an idiot, or a distracted person should be good, if ratified by the General Court. But this provision was dropped from the later revisions, possibly because it was considered contrary to English law.[1]

Simple contracts were in use from the beginning, and it would seem that at first there was little controversy except as to the kind and amount of payment. It was declared, October 18, 1631, that all debts could be paid in corn at the usual price, unless money or beaver had been expressly stipulated.[2] A wider medium of exchange soon became necessary; and it was ordered, October 7, 1640, that no man should be compelled to pay "any debt, legacy, fine or any other payment in money," but that he could pay in "corn, cattle, fish, or other commodities" at a rate fixed by the General Court or, in default of that, at a rate fixed by appraisers. This provision was not to apply to past obligations.[3]

Economic conditions continued to vary, and the provisions made from time to time little more than met the current exigencies. Nothing approaching a permanent regulation was devised until August 22, 1654, when a statute was passed setting forth the kinds of payment and the rights of parties in contracts. It was ordered "that all contracts and engagements for money, corn, cattle or fish" should "be satisfied in kind according to covenant or, in default of the very kind contracted for, in one of the said kinds." Where "payment in kind" was "not made according to covenant, all just damage" sustained thereby was to "be satisfied (together with the

[1] *Bibliog. Sketch*, p. 27.

[2] *Mass. Col. Rec.*, vol. i, p. 92.

[3] *Ibid.*, vol. i, p. 304.

debt)." In no case could a "creditor be forced to take any other commodities for satisfaction of his debt, unless" he had so contracted; but he could imprison the party till satisfaction was made "according to covenant" or "take upon execution such goods, houses, or lands as" should "be to his satisfaction."[1] This act was amended, October 12, 1670, to the effect that "all contracts, agreements, engagements, or covenants for any specie whatsoever" should "be paid in the same specie bargained for."[2]

Servants[3] and workmen were free to contract their services to whomsoever they pleased. In the revisions of 1660 and 1672 it was provided that their wages should be paid in corn, unless they had contracted for some particular payment, in which case they were entitled to compensation for default. The towns were to fix the amount of wages, and both servants and workmen were bound thereby."[4]

A promise to marry was considered binding, and as early as 1633 a breach of promise suit was decided by the court of assistants. It was ordered "that Joyce Bradwicke" should "give unto Alex. Becke the some of xx[s], for promising him marriage without her friends consent & nowe refusing to performe the same."[5] Since parents had to give their consent to the mating of their children, they became parties to the agreement. In 1670 Hope Allen was brought before the court for

[1] *Mass. Col. Rec.*, vol. iv, pt. i, p. 197; *Laws*, 1660–72, p. 183; *Laws*, 1672–86, pp. 120–1.

[2] *Mass. Col. Rec.*, vol. iv, pt. ii, p. 463; *Laws*, 1672–86, p. 121.

[3] Winthrop (Savage), vol. ii, p. 269.

[4] *Laws*, 1660–72, p. 174; *Laws*, 1672–86, p. 105.

[5] *Rec. Assist.*, vol. ii, p. 32; Howard, vol. ii, p. 200.

breaking his word after having consented to his daughter's marriage. He was required "to pay ten pounds as a fine to the country for his irregular procedure," and forty shillings to the disappointed lover.[1]

Toward the end of this period, the court of assistants rendered two noteworthy decisions in regard to contract. It was decided in 1674 that a subsequent contract, whose terms were inconsistent with, and whose parties included the parties to, a former contract, superseded the former contract and rendered it void.[2] Not so reasonable, however, was the doctrine laid down in 1679, when it was held "that the lessor's non-performance of the covenant doth not disoblige the lesse[e]."[3]

PROPERTY

The colonial conceptions of property rights were largely English,[4] but when it came to rights in land there were wide departures from the custom and law of the mother country. As early as May 19, 1629, before the transfer of the government and charter, provision was made for the allotment of land,[5] and further regulations in regard to this matter were adopted in the following December.[6] After the government was established in the colony, the court of assistants made land grants both to towns and to individuals; but it was de-

[1] *Mass. Col. Rec.*, vol. iv, pt. ii, p. 458; Howard, vol. ii, p. 202.

[2] Hutchinson agt. Payne, *Rec. Assist.*, vol. i, p. 28.

[3] Hill agt. Obbinson, *ibid.*, vol. i, p. 151.

[4] Various provisions for taxes (raising of public stock) in *Mass. Col. Rec.*; ordinances in Dedham and other town records; subjects dealt with in *Suffolk Deeds; Title, Charges, Public*, in *Laws*, 1660–72, pp. 133 *et seq.*, and in *Laws*, 1672–86, pp. 22 *et seq.*

[5] *Mass. Col. Rec.*, vol. i, p. 43.

[6] *Ibid.*, vol. i, p. 64.

clared May 14, 1634, among other things, "that none but the General Court hath power to . . . dispose of lands, viz.: to give & confirme proprieties."[1] The following year, however, the towns were given the "power to dispose of their own lands & woods."[2] Thereafter the towns allotted their own lands,[3] but they were limited of course to the portions assigned them by the General Court. From lands not assigned to the several towns the General Court continued to make grants to towns and to individuals.[4]

By order of March 4, 1633, persons were forbidden to buy land of the Indians "without leave from the Court,"[5] and this order was enforced in a case decided in 1639.[6] But a law of June 2, 1641, gave those who had discovered mines a general permission to buy of the Indians the land where such mines were situated.[7] A new element was added, October 11, 1665, to the prohibition in regard to buying Indian lands, when it was interpreted to include as well "grants for a term of years as for ever."[8]

From the beginning the holder or grantee of land had full ownership. There were no feudal tenures, and hence there would naturally be none of the burdens or inci-

[1] *Mass. Col. Rec.*, vol. i, p. 117; *Laws*, 1660–72, p. 141; *Laws*, 1672–86, p. 34.

[2] *Mass. Col. Rec.*, vol. i, p. 172; *Laws*, 1660–72, p. 195; *Laws*, 1672–86, p. 147.

[3] See Dedham and other town records, *passim*.

[4] See *Mass. Col. Rec.*, *passim*.

[5] *Ibid.*, vol. i, p. 112; *Laws*, 1660–72, p. 161; *Laws*, 1672–86, p. 74.

[6] Case of John Bayley, *Rec. Assist.*, vol. ii, p. 83.

[7] *Mass. Col. Rec.*, vol. i, p. 327; *Laws*, 1660–72, p. 181; *Laws*, 1672–86, pp. 116–17.

[8] *Mass. Col. Rec.*, vol. iv, pt. ii, p. 282; *Laws*, 1672–86, p. 75.

dents connected with such tenures; yet these burdens or incidents were expressly forbidden by Liberty 10 and in the subsequent revisions of the laws.[1] The absolute ownership of the holders or grantees of land, both Indians and English, was affirmed October 19, 1652. This act declared "that what lands any of the Indians . . . have by possession or improvement, by subduing the same, they have just right thereunto, according to that in Gen. 1, 28 & chap. 9, 1 and Psal. 115, 16"; and the Indians were to have redress if any one attempted to drive them "from their planting grounds or fishing places." The same act further provided

that all the tract of Land within this jurisdiction, whether already graunted to any English plantations or persons, or to be graunted by this Court (not being under the qualifications of right to the Indians) is, and shall be accounted the just Right of such English as already have, or hereafter shall have graunt of Lands from this Court, and the Authority thereof; from that of Genesis 1, 28 and the Invitation of the Indians.[2]

Although land grants made by public authority were intended by the General Court to confer upon the grantees unconditional estates, doubt seems to have arisen in regard to those made by the towns. An order of May 7, 1651, had provided that conveyances intended to create estates in fee simple should be expressed in these words: "To have & to hold the said House or Land respectively to the Party or Grantee his Heires and Assignes forever,"[3] or in words to like effect. Although it was ex-

[1] *Laws*, 1660–72, p. 168; *Laws*, 1672–86, p. 88.

[2] *Mass. Col. Rec.*, vol. iv, pt. i, pp. 102–3; *Laws*, 1660–72, pp. 160–61; *Laws*, 1672–86, p. 74.

[3] *Mass. Col. Rec.*, vol. iv, pt. i, p. 39; *Laws*, 1660–72, p. 140; *Laws*, 1672–86, p. 32.

pressly stated that this order should not extend "to any land granted or to be granted by the Inhabitants of a town," question seems to have arisen whether the words "Heires and Assignes forever" were essential in a town grant to create an estate in fee simple. It was declared, therefore, March 18, 1684, that all grants of land made by the General Court or by the towns were to be held by the grantees as estates in fee simple, unless it were expressly stated "otherwise, *viz: to be for Term of Life or for Term of Years, or during pleasure* or the like." This provision was to apply to former as well as to subsequent grants.[1]

Provision was made for acquiring title by undisputed possession for a period of years. An order of October 19, 1652,[2] had made a number of regulations in regard to conveyances. These were qualified to a certain ex-extent by another order of May 6, 1657, to the effect that any one who had possession of land before October 19, 1652 and continued in such possession, undisputed, for five years, should have title.[3] In answer to a question submitted May 15, 1672, the General Court interpreted this statute to include "the confirmation of land to the possessor where the grant of the said land was to another person, & the possessor [has] nothing to show for the allienation thereof but his possession."[4]

When a proprietor's land adjoined waters where the tide ebbed and flowed not over a hundred rods, the proprietor, according to a statute dated 1647, was to own

[1] *Mass. Col. Rec.*, vol. v, pp. 470–471; *Laws*, 1672–86, pp. 353–4.

[2] *Mass. Col. Rec.*, vol. iv, pt. i, p. 101; *Laws*, 1660–72, p. 140; *Laws*, 1672–86, p. 32.

[3] *Mass. Col. Rec.*, vol. iv, pt. i, p. 288; *Laws*, 1660–72, p. 185; *Laws*, 1672–86, pp. 123–4.

[4] *Mass. Col. Rec.*, vol. iv, pt. ii, p. 515.

to low-water mark. But he was not to interfere with the passage of boats or other vessels to the houses and lands of others.[1] In answer to a question submitted October 17, 1649, the General Court declared that this law would not render void a previous town order, setting apart about twenty acres lying between the salt marshes and the low-water mark, "for the use of the whole town to be improved for thatched houses."[2] And it answered another question, May 19, 1669, by declaring that towns could reserve land along the tide waters in making their own grants, in which case the adjoining proprietor could not claim further than had been assigned him.[3]

FAMILY

There were a number of innovations in family law. Marriage became a civil institution, and the magistrate replaced the minister at the ceremony.[4] But before the relation could be entered into, several preliminary steps were necessary. Among other things, the consent of the girl's parents or friends was required. In 1640 a lover was bound to his good behavior for "seeking to get a mayde without her friends' consent," and any resumption of his suit was "to bee accounted a breach of the good behavior."[5] Before many years had passed this attitude of the court found its way into statute: November 11, 1647, the General Court, after asserting the right of parents to dispose of their children in marriage, declared that any one who sought the hand of a maid in

[1] *Laws*, 1660–72, p. 170; *Laws*, 1672–86, p. 91.

[2] *Mass. Col. Rec.*, vol. ii, p. 284.

[3] *Ibid.*, vol. iv, pt. ii, pp. 427–8.

[4] Hutchinson, vol. i, p. 392.

[5] Case of Thomas Baguley, *Rec. Assist.*, vol. ii, p. 97.

marriage, before securing the consent of "her parents or Governors, or in the absence of such, of the nearest magistrate," should be fined five pounds for the first offense, ten pounds for the second, and be imprisoned for the third.[1] That this provision did not remain a dead letter is shown by a number of convictions which followed.[2]

Although the consent of parents was required, yet, according to Liberty 83, if children were denied timely and convenient marriage, they could "complaine to Authority for redresse."[3] By a law dated 1646, the age of consent to marriage was fixed in the case of women at sixteen.[4]

Consanguinity, according to Hutchinson, was settled in the same degrees as in English and Levitical law.[5] But the marriage of first cousins, by affinity as well as by blood, and marriage with a dead wife's sister were strongly opposed.[6] In the former provision the colonists went beyond the laws of England,[7] and in the latter they were more stringent than the Mosaic code. The only legal declaration on this subject, however, was that of May 31, 1670, when the General Court, in answer to a question, denounced marriage with a dead wife's sister.[8]

Publication of intention was necessary. By order of

[1] *Mass. Col. Rec.*, vol. ii, p. 207; *Laws*, 1660–72, p. 172; *Laws*, 1672–86, p. 101.

[2] *Mass. Col. Rec.*, vol. iv, pt. i, p. 147; Howard, vol. ii, p. 166.

[3] *Laws*, 1660–72, p. 137; *Laws*, 1672–86, p. 28; Howard, vol. ii, p. 166.

[4] *Laws*, 1660–72, p. 137; *Laws*, 1672–86, p. 28.

[5] Hutchinson, vol. i, p. 393.

[6] Howard, vol. ii, p. 212.

[7] *Ibid.*

[8] *Mass. Col. Rec.*, vol. iv, pt. ii, p. 454; *Laws*, 1672–86, p. 102. Misdated in the text of the law; it should be 1670 in place of 1679.

September 9, 1639, this had to be made at three separate public lectures or town meetings in the town where each of the parties resided. In towns having no public lectures, fourteen days' notice was to be given in writing on a post standing in public view and used for that purpose only.[1]

From the first it was the custom for the magistrates to perform the ceremony, but commissions were granted from time to time empowering other persons in the remote towns to solemnize marriage.[2] No one might act in this capacity without authority. As early as March 1, 1630, the constable of Dorchester, "for taking upon him to marry" a couple, was fined five pounds and ordered to be imprisoned until he paid the fine.[3] Self-marriage was not tolerated. The case of Governor Bellingham, who entered into a private marriage in 1641, is in point. Bellingham had courted and won a young lady who resided at his house, after he had consented that another should be her suitor. "Two errors more," says Winthrop, "he committed upon it. 1. That he would not have his contract published where he dwelt, contrary to an order of court. 2. That he married himself, contrary to the constant practice of the country."[4]

The attitude of the colonists toward ecclesiastical marriage is shown in an incident which took place in 1647. The magistrates forbade Hubbard's preaching at a wedding in Boston, although the parties were members of his church. Two reasons were assigned for this. In

[1] *Mass. Col. Rec.*, vol. i, p. 275; *Laws*, 1660–72, pp. 171–2; *Laws*, 1672–86, p. 101. Sometimes suspended in special cases; *cf. Mass. Col. Rec.*. vol. ii, p. 46; Howard, vol. ii, p. 145.

[2] *Mass. Col. Rec., passim;* Hutchinson, vol. i, p. 392.

[3] *Rec. Assist.*, vol. ii, p. 10.

[4] Winthrop (Savage), vol. ii, pp. 51–2; Howard, vol. ii, pp. 210–11.

the first place, they knew Hubbard was not very friendly toward the government, and, since he was a bold man, they feared he might speak his mind. In the second place, they did not wish "to bring in the English custom of ministers performing" marriage ceremonies, and they feared that sermons at weddings might have that tendency. If ministers were present on such occasions, however, they were permitted to "bestow a word of exortation." [1]

Such customs, though binding, were not immediately enacted into statutes. This was doubtless due to the fact that the colonists thought a statute on the subject would be repugnant to the laws of England, and, therefore, a transgression of the charter. Winthrop, in 1639, after expressing this view, continued as follows:

> But to raise up laws by practice and custom had been no transgression; as in our church discipline, and in matters of marriage, to make a law, that marriage should not be solemnized by ministers, is repugnant to the laws of England; but to bring it to a custom by practice for the magistrates to perform it, is no law made repugnant.[2]

A statute on the subject was finally passed: it is contained in the revisions of 1660 and 1672, and is dated 1646. It reads:

> As the Ordinance of Marriage is honorable amongst all, so should it be accordingly solemnized. It is therefore Ordered by this Court and Authority thereof, That no person whatsoever in this Jurisdiction, shall joyne any persons to gether in Marriage, but the Magistrates, or such other as the General

[1] Winthrop (Savage), vol. ii, p. 382: Howard, vol. ii, p. 127.

[2] Winthrop (Savage), vol. i, p. 389; *cf.* Morton, *New English Canaan* (Prince Soc. Pub., vol. ix, Boston, 1883), pp. 330-1.

> Court, or Court of Assistants shall Authorize in such place, where no Magistrate is neer. Nor shal any joyne themselves in Marriage, but before some Magistrate or person authorized as aforesaid. Nor shal any Magistrate, or other person authorized as aforesaid, joyne any persons together in Marriage, or suffer them to joyne together in Marriage in their presence, before the parties to be married have been published according to Law.[1]

Provisions were made from time to time for the registration of marriages as well as births and deaths.[2]

Law and custom did not cease to operate at the conclusion of the ceremony. The married pair were answerable to authority for their conduct toward each other. Liberty 80 provided that every married woman should be free from bodily correction by her husband, unless it were in self-defense upon her assault. In case such correction were needed, complaint was to be made to authority, from which alone she should receive it.[3] This provision was continued, in spirit, in the later revisions, to the effect that neither party should strike the other, on pain of fine or corporal punishment.[4] The courts did not hesitate to attempt to adjust family differences. In 1638 a case of wife-beating was before the court of assistants,[5] and in 1641 a husband was enjoined to return

[1] *Laws*, 1660–72, p. 172; *Laws*, 1672–86, p. 102.

[2] *Mass. Col. Rec.*, vol. i, p. 276; vol. ii, p. 15; vol. iv, pt. i, p. 290; *Laws*, 1660-72, p. 188; *Laws*, 1672–86, p. 130; Howard, vol. ii, pp. 145–6.

[3] This was "to put at rest the question whether it was lawful, as it was supposed to be in England, for a man to whip his wife with a stick, 'if no bigger than his little finger.'" Howe, *The Puritan Republic of the Massachusetts Bay in New England*, Indianapolis, n. d. (copyright, 1899), p. 55; *cf.* Hutchinson, vol, i, p. 392.

[4] *Laws*, 1660–72, p. 171; *Laws*, 1672–86, p. 101.

[5] Case of Henry Sewall, *Rec. Assist.*, vol. ii, p. 74.

to his mate.[1] The General Court in 1665 ordered a man and his wife to live together as such "on the penalty of forty pounds on his part, & imprisonment on hers;"[2] and in 1669 it issued a similar command to another couple.[3] In regard to Hugh March and Dorcas, his wife, the court of assistants decided, September 9, 1678, that they could not "still lawfully live as man & wife;"[4] but the General Court reversed this decision on the 7th of the following October and enjoined Hugh March to return to his wife and "observe & fulfill the marriage covenant according to his engagement."[5]

Divorces were granted where the courts found adequate grounds. Although the statutes are silent on this subject, there were several causes recognized as sufficient. Hutchinson mentions female adultery,[6] desertion for a year or two without intention to return, and cruel usage by the husband.[7] Cotton Mather adds that in case of impotency "the *marriage*" should "be declared a *nullity*."[8] These causes were assigned as grounds for the various decrees issued in the courts. Marriage was, of course, declared void where the man had a former wife.[9] The cases that arose from time to time will not

[1] Case of Edward Adams, *Rec. Assist.*, vol. ii, p. 105.

[2] *Mass. Col. Rec.*, vol. iv, pt. ii, p. 288.

[3] *Ibid.*, vol. iv, pt. ii, pp. 426–7.

[4] *Rec. Assist.*, vol. i, p. 127.

[5] *Mass. Col. Rec.*, vol. v, p. 205.

[6] Since adultery was a death crime, divorce would be necessary only when the wife was outside the jurisdiction. Male adultery was not considered a cause for divorce. Hutchinson, vol. i, p. 393.

[7] Hutchinson, vol. ii, p. 393.

[8] Mather, *Magnalia*, vol. ii, p. 217.

[9] Case of James Luxford, *Mass. Col. Rec.*, vol. i, p. 286; *Rec. Assist.*, vol. ii, p. 89; Elizabeth Frier agt. John Richardson, *Mass. Col. Rec.*, vol. ii, p. 86.

be discussed here,[1] but two decisions are worthy of note because of the peculiar language used. In 1652 the General Court granted "the petitioner liberty to marry when God by his providence shall affoord hir an apportunity;"[2] and in 1670 the same Court declared "that the petitioner marrying any other man shall not be indangered thereby as a transgressour of our lawes."[3]

Although cases of divorce properly belonged to the court of assistants,[4] with appeal to the General Court,[5] the latter often took original jurisdiction of such cases on petition. Some of the decrees, accordingly, were issued by the court of assistants and some by the General Court. The divorces granted were not *a mensa et thoro* but *a vinculo*.[6]

Boys reached their majority at the age of twenty-one and girls at the age of eighteen.[7] Certain duties, however, were imposed, and certain capacities were accorded, during minority. At the age of sixteen boys were liable for military training,[8] and girls could give their consent in marriage.[9] Children over fourteen could select their own guardians, where guardians were required.[10] Al-

[1] For full discussion of cases, see Howard, vol. ii, pp. 330–6.

[2] *Mass. Col. Rec.*, vol. iv, pt. i, p. 89.

[3] *Ibid.*, pt. ii, p. 465.

[4] Noble, *Pub. Col. Soc. of Mass.*, vol. iii, p. 52; *Bibliog. Sketch*, p. 103, note; *Laws*, 1660–72, p. 143; *Laws*, 1672–86, p. 36.

[5] *Bibliog. Sketch*, p. 101, note; Howard, vol. ii, pp. 334–5.

[6] Hutchinson, vol. i, p. 393; Howard, vol. ii, p. 339.

[7] *Laws*, 1660–72, p. 136; *Laws*, 1672–86, p. 26. The age for transacting business was twenty-one. Liberty 53; *Laws*, 1660–72, pp. 121, 137; *Laws*, 1672–86, pp. 1, 27, 28.

[8] *Laws*, 1660–72, p. 177; *Laws*, 1672–86, p. 109.

[9] *Laws*, 1660–72, p. 137; *Laws*, 1672–86, p. 28.

[10] *Laws*, 1660–72, p. 121; *Laws*, 1672–86, p. 1. The mother could be appointed on the death of the father. *Abstracts from Wills, etc.* (Hist. Coll. Essex Institute, vol. iv), p. 26.

though minors were under the authority of their parents or guardians, they were permitted by Liberty 83 to complain to authority for redress in case of cruelty or denial of their rights. Orphans, according to Liberty 84, could not be disposed of except by authority of some court.[1]

The term "apprentice" was often applied to a child bound out to some responsible person.[2] Little distinction seems to have existed between the terms "ward" and "apprentice," except that the latter may have been used where a definite period of years was specified. They were doubtless used interchangeably. Children bound out were sometimes called "servants."[3] It may be stated with safety that no fine legal distinctions were drawn between children, wards, apprentices and minor servants. All lived under family government, and had in the main the duties and rights of children.

Many laws were passed for the education and training of children and the religious instruction of servants. In case of neglect on the part of the person responsible, after admonition, his children were to be apprenticed to another. Disobedient children and servants could be punished by civil authority, either corporally up to ten stripes, or in some other way.[4]

As already stated, the relation between master and servant was established by contract. This relation could

[1] *Laws*, 1660–72, p. 137; *Laws*, 1672–86, p. 28.

[2] *Rec. Assist.*, vol. ii, pp. 17, 22, 25, 41, 117. A minor might apprentice himself in certain cases, just as he could choose a guardian. *Records*, vol. ii, p. 117. Indian children might be apprenticed. *Mass. Col. Rec.*, vol. v, p. 136; *Laws*, 1672–86, pp. 251–2.

[3] *Mass. Col. Rec.*, vol. iv, pt. i, p. 113.

[4] *Ibid.*, vol. ii, pp. 6–7, 9; vol. iv, pt. ii, pp. 395–6; vol. v, p. 59; *Laws*, 1660–72, pp. 136, 139, 260; *Laws*, 1672–86, pp. 26, 27, 149, 150.

not be terminated by mutual consent before the time of service had expired. A law to this effect was passed in 1636;[1] but it is contained neither in the *Body of Liberties* nor in the revision of 1660, nor in that of 1672. Upon this point there were, however, several decisions, some of them rendered after the *Body of Liberties* was adopted. Two persons were fined in 1639 for releasing servants before the expiration of their time.[2] Consent of the court was required. In 1642 the transfer of a servant from one master to another was permitted,[3] and in 1644 a person was granted leave to set his servant free.[4] The last case indicates that the rule was in force down to that date, at least. According to Liberty 86, no person could hire his servant out to another for more than a year, nor could this be done by the executor or administrator after the master's death, except with the consent of civil authority.

Servants were protected against cruel treatment. Liberty 87 declared that if a person wounded or maimed his servant, except by accident, he should let him go free and give him such other recompense as the court should allow.[5] Masters had been brought to justice before this law was passed. For abusing his servant a master was fined in 1638.[6] An abused servant was transferred in 1640 from one master to another;[7] and in the same year

[1] *Mass. Col. Rec.*, vol. i, p. 186.

[2] Case of Captain Staugton, *Rec. Assist.*, vol. ii, p. 84; Case of Ralph Allen, *ibid.*, vol. ii, p. 84.

[3] Case of Elisha Jackson, *ibid.*, vol. ii, p. 119.

[4] Case of John Gore, *Mass. Col. Rec.*, vol. ii, p. 67.

[5] *Laws*, 1660–72, p. 175; *Laws*, 1672–86, p. 105.

[6] Case of John Poole, *Rec. Assist.*, vol. ii, p. 80.

[7] Case of Samuel Hefford, *Mass. Col. Rec.*, vol. i, p. 311.

a master was fined and bound to his good behavior for cruel usage of his servant.[1]

In some respects the duties of servants were regulated by law. An order of September 7, 1630, prohibited servants from carrying on any business whatsoever without the consent of their masters, "under paine of fyne & corporall punishment, att the discression of the Court."[2] The servant must render to his master due respect and obedience. In 1631 a servant was whipped "for his ill speeches & misbehavior towards his master;"[3] and in 1641 a servant received a severe whipping for reviling the master and "refusing to obey his lawful commands."[4] Whipping was the usual punishment, but in 1643 a servant who had gone so far as to strike his master was sentenced to imprisonment.[5]

Runaway servants, according to an order of September 3, 1635, were to be brought back at the public expense.[6] They were punished, too, for running away. In such a case, in 1633, a severe whipping was imposed.[7] Other punishments were sometimes added; in 1635, the offending servant was whipped and the time of servitude was extended;[8] and in 1639 the servant was sentenced to receive a severe whipping and afterward to be kept in chains. In the last case, however, the servant had com-

[1] Case of Christopher Graunt, *Rec. Assist.*, vol. ii, p. 103.

[2] *Mass. Col. Rec.*, vol. i, p. 76; *Laws*, 1660–72, p. 174; *Laws*, 1672–86, p. 104.

[3] Case of Frauncis Perry, *Rec. Assist.*, vol. ii, p. 18.

[4] Case of Richard Wilson, *ibid.*, vol. ii, p. 104.

[5] Case of Thomas Bauldwin, *ibid.*, vol. ii, p. 134.

[6] *Mass. Col. Rec.*, vol. i, p. 157; *Laws*, 1660–72, p. 174; *Laws*, 1672–86, p. 104.

[7] Case of John Sayles, *Rec. Assist.*, vol. ii, p. 40.

[8] Case of Mary, servant, *ibid.*, vol. ii, p. 57.

mitted two offenses: he had stolen and had run away.[1] Severe whipping seems to have been the usual penalty. If a servant fled from the cruelty of his master, he was to be protected, according to Liberty 85, until his case could be investigated.[2]

Diligence in service was not to be without just reward, nor indolence without due penalty. Liberty 88 declared that servants who had been faithful for seven years should not be sent away empty, but that those who had been unfaithful, "notwithstanding the good usage of their masters," should "not be dismissed" until they had "made satisfaction according to the judgment of Authority."[3]

SUCCESSION

The right to dispose of property by a last will was judicially recognized before there was any express statute on the subject. It was not long, however, until this right was affirmed by legislative authority. Liberty 11 declared that all persons over twenty-one[4] and of sound mind, even if "excommunicate or condemned," should "have full power and liberty to make wills and testaments."[5]

Wills were usually witnessed by two or more persons, who subscribed their names;[6] and, according to the re-

[1] Case of John Neal, *ibid.*, vol. ii, p. 86.

[2] *Laws*, 1660–72, p. 175; *Laws*, 1672–86, p. 105.

[3] *Laws*, 1660–72, p. 175; *Laws*, 1672–86, p. 105. Slavery existed to a certain extent in the colony. See *Mass. Col. Rec.*, vol. v, p. 136; *Laws*, 1660–72, p. 125; *Laws*, 1672–86, p. 10; Howard, vol. ii, pp. 217–8.

[4] The will of a minor was rejected in 1646. *Mass. Col. Rec.*, vol. ii, p. 183.

[5] *Laws*, 1660–72, p. 121: *Laws*, 1672–86, p. 1.

[6] See *Mass. Col. Rec.*, vol. i, p. 153; Winthrop (Savage), vol. ii, pp.

visions of 1660 and 1672, the oaths of two or more witnesses were necessary to prove a will before the court.[1] Already had provision been made, by order of October 17, 1649, for the speedy probate of wills and the speedy distribution of the property of those who died intestate.[2]

Technical points frequently came up for judicial decision. In 1652 the General Court admitted a copy of a will when the original had been lost.[3] In 1681 the court of assistants decided that, in case a man gave "his daughter a legacy," calling her in the will "his daughter the wife of such a man, & she" died "without issue before the time of payment," the legacy would not belong to the husband after her death.[4]

The power of disposing of property by will was not without limitation. Liberty 79 provided that, if any man at his death did not leave his wife a competent portion of his estate, she should be relieved "upon just complaint to the Generall Court." This is not contained in the revisions, but is continued in spirit in the law of dower, probably passed in 1647[5] and amended May 2, 1649.[6] As the law was incorporated in the the revisions, the widow was to have a life-time right

to one third part of all such Houses, Lands, Tenements and

436-41; *Abstract of Wills* (Hist. Colls. Essex Institute, vols. i to iv). In case of severe illness, wills seem to have been valid, although not signed by the testator, if he were still able to certify to the writing. *Ibid.*, vol. iv, p. 171.

[1] *Laws*, 1660-72, p. 201; *Laws*, 1672-86, p. 158.

[2] *Mass. Col. Rec.*, vol. ii, pp. 287-8; *Laws*, 1660-72, p. 201; *Laws*, 1672-86, p. 157.

[3] *Mass. Col. Rec.*, vol. iv, pt. i, p. 118.

[4] Chapman agt. Barry, *Rec. Assist.*, vol. i, p. 205.

[5] *Bibliog. Sketch*, pp. 26, 28.

[6] *Mass. Col. Rec.*, vol. ii, p. 281.

Hereditaments . . . free . . . from all titles, debts, rents, charges, judgments, executions & other incumbrances whatsoever, had made or suffered by her husband, during the said marriage, [unless she had given her consent] by writing under her hand, & acknowledged before some Magistrate or others Authorized thereunto which [should] barr her from any right or interest in such estate.

A divorced wife was to have full right to dower when she was not at fault. These provisions were not to extend to sales or conveyances made before the last of November, 1647.[1]

In 1658 the General Court refused to grant dower where property had been taken on a mortgage given in satisfaction of a debt and was in possession of the mortgagee's children.[2] This was a complicated and exceptional case, and does not indicate that the law of dower was disregarded. On the contrary, in 1679 the thirds were given by the court of assistants.[3]

In case a person died intestate, the eldest son, according to Liberty 81,[4] was to have a double portion of the property; and by Liberty 82, where there were no sons, the daughters were to share equally. The court, however, had power in both cases to "judge otherwise" upon sufficient grounds.[5] From an answer given to a petitioner in 1679 by the General Court, it would seem that in the absence of children the widow would receive a lifetime right to the whole estate, with power to will one-

[1] *Laws*, 1660–72, p. 146; *Laws*, 1672–86, p. 42.

[2] Case of Mrs. Foote, *Mass. Col. Rec.*, vol. iv, pt. i, p. 352.

[3] Dower to the widow Hill, *Rec. Assist.*, vol. i, p. 147.

[4] Probably a way of avoiding the full effects of primogeniture. See *Hutchinson Papers*, vol. i, p. 235.

[5] *Laws*, 1660–72, p. 201; *Laws*, 1672–86, p. 158.

half of it as she pleased, the other half to go to the husband's relatives after her death.[1]

It was ordered, May 24, 1677, that, when a person died intestate and his property was not sufficient to satisfy his creditors, it should be divided amongst them proportionately. But the creditors had to make their claim within twelve months, unless the county court saw fit to extend the time.[2]

Although feudal burdens upon inheritance had been forbidden by Liberty 10, an order of November 4, 1646, declared "that where no heire or owner of houses, Lands, tenements, goods or chattles" could "be found, they" should "be seized to the public Treasury, till such heirs or owners" should "make due claim thereto, unto whom they" should "be restored upon just and reasonable terms."[3]

What rights belonged to an alien heir appearing by his attorney came up for consideration in 1673. The General Court referred the matter to a committee with instructions to investigate the law of England on the subject and decide the case. The committee was also to draw up an order in respect to the trust and power of guardians and present the same to the Court.[4] This indicates the tendency to consult English precedents in difficult questions.

[1] *Mass. Col. Rec.*, vol. v, p. 224.

[2] *Ibid.*, vol. v, pp. 134-5; *Laws*, 1672-86, pp. 250-1.

[3] *Mass. Col. Rec.*, vol. ii, p. 182; *Laws*, 1660-72, p. 150; *Laws*, 1672-86, p. 49.

[4] *Mass. Col. Rec.*, vol. iv, pt. ii, pp. 554-5.

CONCLUSION

At first, as we have seen, the entire civil authority was concentrated in the hands of the governor and magistrates. It was not long, however, until the General Court assumed legislative power, defined the jurisdiction of the court of assistants and further perfected the machinery of justice. The representative system came into use, the deputies and assistants separated into two houses, and the speaker became an equal factor with the governor in legislation. The distribution of powers, however, was not accompanied by a corresponding division of personnel. The governor and magistrates were the upper house of the legislature; they acted as an executive council; and, in their judicial capacity, they sat as the court of assistants. The magistrates also assisted as judges in the various county courts and attended to numerous local affairs of a judicial or administrative character. These facts tended to arrest the development of any sharp distinction between legislation and court decision, since it devolved for the most part upon a portion of the legislative body to interpret and enforce the statutes they had helped to enact.

The government fostered and protected the church and received moral support in return. The sphere of the former was the outer, that of the latter the inner man. No portion of church organization, therefore, was exempt from secular supervision and control. Doctrine and discipline received the sanction and support of law, and heresy in the church became treason to the state.

Under such a system there could be no serious conflict between secular and ecclesiastical power; for the religious organization recognized by the government was the church, and there could be no other.

There was no professionally trained class of attorneys, and English legal treatises were cited for illustration, not as authority. English precedents were followed in civil and criminal procedure. There was presentment by a grand jury in criminal cases and trial by a petty jury in both civil and criminal cases.

The criminal laws were based largely upon the Mosaic code, especially where the death penalty was prescribed. The manner of executing the death sentence, however, was English, not Jewish. For the lesser offenses ignominious punishments were often imposed in order to humiliate the offender. Crime was a sin and repentance was necessary. In criminal actions private wrongs were often recognized and redressed.

Deeds followed the English form, but registration was required for their validity. Feudal burdens and incidents were forbidden. Land was held in fee simple, and a proprietor's right extended to low-tide mark. Marriage became a civil institution, and the magistrate replaced the minister at the ceremony. Questions of divorce were settled by the civil and not by the ecclesiastical authority. Divorces were *a vinculo* and not *a mensa et thoro*; but they did not defeat dower if the wife were not at fault. The right to dispose of one's property by a last will was recognized. English primogeniture was avoided by giving the eldest son a double portion. In the absence of sons, the daughters shared equally, and, in the absence of children, the widow received life-right to all the estate and power to dispose of half of it by will.

Owing doubtless to the conditions under which they lived, the colonists showed some tendency to revert to early law. In some matters, at least, their points of view and the resulting legislation or custom were those of a society more primitive than that of contemporary England. The imperfect development of government threw upon the whole body of freemen functions which, in England, were beginning to be assumed by special agencies of the state. The general duty of active co-operation in the defense of the frontier and in the maintenance of the peace was recognized in English law; in England also, for example, failure to join in the hue and cry was punishable, for there also an efficient police was yet to be developed; but in the colony active assistance in such emergencies seems to have been more rigorously exacted. In judicial proceedings the jury played a less passive part than in contemporary English courts; it assumed a more independent attitude, particularly in the interpretation of the law; so that the colonial court suggests, in some respects, the mediæval German *Schöffen-Gericht.*[1] Costs, although ultimately assessed against either party at the pleasure of the court, appear primarily, in some of the colonial laws, as fees due from the plaintiff, and were measured, to some extent, by the amount of damages recovered—a system which reminds us of the relation between the composition paid to the plaintiff and the fine paid to the court in old German law, where the fine was a quota of the total award and was originally, as Brunner maintains, a fee paid by the plaintiff for the assistance of the court.[2] The colonial

[1] *Cf.* Hartmann, *Die Strafrechtspflege in Amerika* (Berlin, 1906), pp. 72 *et seq.*

[2] Brunner, *Deutsche Rechtsgeschichte* (Leipzig, 1887), vol. i, sec. 21, p. 165.

attorney, at the outset, was a person very like the old German "forspeaker."[1] The application of substantially similar rules as regarded children, wards, apprentices and minor servants carries us back to the early, solidary household. A reversion also was the practice, lamented by the legally trained Lechford, of terminating cases at one court.[2] It is not intimated that such reversions were deliberate: they were due, of course, to colonial conditions. In some respects, however, the colonists were in advance of the mother country, *e. g.*, in land tenures and in matrimonial institutions.

The colonists did not consider English law binding. The statutes passed by the General Court were to them the positive, and the Scriptures the subsidiary law. Just so much of the English law was adopted, therefore, as the General Court chose to incorporate in its orders, or this court and the other judicial authorities saw fit to recognize in their decisions.[3] In place of bringing with them to America the general principles of the common law, claiming it as their heritage, and applying it where the circumstances permitted, the colonists united three elements in their legal system: (1) They brought with them, in a general way, English institutions, judicial procedure, legal forms, and, to a certain extent, personal and property rights. (2) They drew from the Mosaic code and other portions of the Bible certain notions of theocratic government, moral and religious duties, and criminal liability. (3) To these they added a colonial

[1] Brunner, *op. cit.*, vol. ii, sec. 100, pp. 349 *et seq.*; Pollock and Maitland, *History of English Law* (Cambridge, 1895), vol. i, pp. 190 *et seq.*

[2] *Cf.* XII Tables, 1, 9: "Sol occasus suprema tempestas esto."

[3] And even where the decisions were in accordance with English law, they were often based by the courts upon the authority of tha Scriptures.

element, made up of laws and customs that were in part somewhat archaic and in part far in advance of the times. These three elements, the English, the Jewish, and the colonial, were curiously blended, producing in effect what was largely a new legal system. Notwithstanding opposition from a minority, which demanded the adoption of English law, the Puritans successfully maintained their position until the government under the first charter came to an end.

SELECTED BIBLIOGRAPHY

I. Sources

A. *Legal*

Abstracts from Wills, Inventories, etc. In Historical Collections of the Essex Institute, vols. i-v.

Calendar of State Papers. Colonial Series, 1574-1698. London, 1860-1905.

Cambridge and Saybrook Platforms of Church Discipline. Boston, 1829.

Colonial Laws of Massachusetts, 1660-1672. Published under supervision of William H. Whitmore. Boston, 1889.

Colonial Laws of Massachusetts, 1672-86. Published under supervision of William H. Whitmore. Boston, 1887.

Early Records of Groton, Massachusetts. Groton, 1880.

Early Records of Lancaster, Massachusetts. Lancaster, 1884.

Early Records of the Town of Dedham, Massachusetts. Dedham, 1892-4.

Essex County Court Records. In Historical Collections of the Essex Institute, vols. vii viii.

Macdonald, William. *Select Charters and other Documents, illustrative of American History.* New York, 1904.

Poore, Ben: Perley. *Federal and State Constitutions, Colonial Charters, and other Organic Laws of the United States* (2 parts). Washington, 1878.

Proprietors' Records of the Town of Mendon, Massachusetts, 1667-1816. Boston, 1899.

Records of the Court of Assistants, 1630-1692 (2 vols.). Printed under supervision of John Noble. Boston, 1901-4.

Records of the Governor and Company of the Massachusetts Bay in New England (5 vols.). Ed. by Nathaniel B. Shurtleff. Boston, 1853-4.

Records of the Town of Cambridge, 1630-1703. Cambridge, 1901.

Register Book of Lands and Houses in "New Towne" and Cambridge, called "Proprietors' Records." Cambridge, 1896.

Suffolk Deeds (14 vols.). Boston, 1880-1906.

Watertown Records. Watertown, Massachusetts, 1894.

B. *Contemporary Literature*

Child, Major John. *New-England's Jonas cast up at London,* 1647. Boston, 1869.

Clark, John. *Ill News from New-England*, 1652. In Collections of the Massachusetts Historical Society, 4th series, vol. ii.

Cotton, John. *An Abstract of the Laws of New England, as they are now Established*. In Collections of the Massachusetts Historical Society, 1st series, vol. v, pp. 173-192.

Cotton, John. *The Keys of the Kingdom of Heaven*. Boston, 1852.

Dunton, John. *Letters written from New-England*. Prince Society Publications, vol. iii. Boston, 1867.

Good News from New-England. In Collections of the Massachusetts Historical Society, 4th series, vol. i, pp. 195-218.

Historical Collections of the Essex Institute (45 vols.). Salem, 1859-1909.

Hooker, Thomas, and Cotton, John. *A Survey of the Summe of Church-Discipline*. London, 1648.

Hubbard, Rev. William. *A General History of New England*. In Collections of the Massachusetts Historical Society, 2nd series, vols. v, vi.

Hutchinson Papers. Prince Society Publications, vol. ii. Albany, 1865.

Johnson, Edward. *Wonder-Working Providence of Sions Saviour in New England*. In Collections of the Massachusetts Historical Society, 2nd series, vols. ii, iii, iv, vii, viii.

Lechford, Thomas. *Plain Dealing*. In Collections of the Massachusetts Historical Society, 3rd series, vol. iii. Also ed. by J. Hammond Trumbull. Boston, 1867.

Lechford, Thomas. *Note-book* (1638-41). Cambridge, 1885.

Mather, Cotton. *Magnalia Christi Americana* (2 vols.). Hartford, 1820.

Mather Papers, with Appendix. In Collections of the Massachusetts Historical Society, 4th series, vol. viii.

Morton, Thomas. *New English Canaan*. Prince Society Publications, vol. ix. Boston, 1883.

Sewell, Samuel. *Diary of Samuel Sewell*. In Collections of the Massachusetts Historical Society, 5th series, vols. v, vi, vii.

Ward, Rev. Nathaniel. *The Simple Cobler*. Ed. by David Pulsifer. Boston, 1843.

Winthrop, John. *The History of New England* (2 vols.). Ed. by James Savage. Boston, 1853. Also in Original Narratives of Early American History. Ed. by James Kendall Hosmer. New York, 1908.

Winthrop, John. *A Modell of Christian Charity*. In Collections of the Massachusetts Historical Society, 3d series, vol. vii.

Young, Alexander. *Chronicles of the First Planters of the Colony of Massachusetts Bay*. Boston, 1846.

II. Secondary Authorities

Bradford, Alden. *History of Massachusetts for two hundred years, 1620–1820.* Boston, 1835.

Davis, Andrew McFarland. *The Law of Adultery and Ignominious Punishments.* Worcester, Massachusetts, 1895.

Doyle, J. A. *The Puritan Colonies* (2 vols.). London, 1887.

Eliot, Rev. John. *Ecclesiastical History of Massachusetts.* In Collections of the Massachusetts Historical Society, 1st series, vols. vii, ix, x; 2nd series, vol. i.

Ellis, George E. *The Puritan Age and Rule.* Boston and New York, 1888.

Felt, Joseph B. *Annals of Salem* (2 vols.). Salem, 1845–9.

Felt, Joseph B. *The Ecclesiastical History of New England* (2 vols.). Boston, 1855–62.

Howard, George Elliott. *A History of Matrimonial Institutions*, vol. ii. Chicago and London, 1904.

Howe, Daniel Wait. *The Puritan Republic of the Massachusetts Bay in New England.* Indianapolis, n. d. (copyright, 1899.)

Hutchinson, Thomas. *The History of the Colony of Massachusetts Bay* (3 vols.). London, 1765.

Memorial History of Boston, vols. i, ii. Ed. by Justin Winsor. Boston, 1880–81.

Narrative and Critical History of America, vol. iii. Ed. by Justin Winsor. Boston and New York, n. d. (copyright, 1884.)

Noble, John. *Notes on the Trial and Punishment of Crimes.* Publications of the Colonial Society of Massachusetts, vol. iii, pp. 51–66.

Oliver, Peter. *The Puritan Commonwealth.* Boston, 1856.

Osgood, Herbert L. *The American Colonies in the Seventeenth Century* (3 vols.). New York, 1904–7.

Palfrey, John Gorham. *History of New England* (5 vols.). Boston, 1858–90.

Reinsch, Paul Samuel. *English Common Law in the Early American Colonies.* Bulletin of the University of Wisconsin, Madison, Wis., 1899.

Waters, Thomas F. *Ipswich in the Massachusetts Bay Colony.* Ipswich, 1905.

Washburn, Emory. *Sketches of the Judicial History of Massachusetts from 1630 to the Revolution in 1775.* Boston, 1840.

Willard, Joseph. *An Address to the Members of the Bar of Worcester County, Massachusetts.* Lancaster, 1830.

Whitmore, William H. *A Bibliographical Sketch of the Laws of Massachusetts Colony.* Boston, 1890.

Bei Fragen zur Produktsicherheit wenden Sie sich bitte an:
If you have any questions regarding product safety,
please contact:

Walter de Gruyter GmbH
Genthiner Straße 13
10785 Berlin
productsafety@degruyterbrill.com